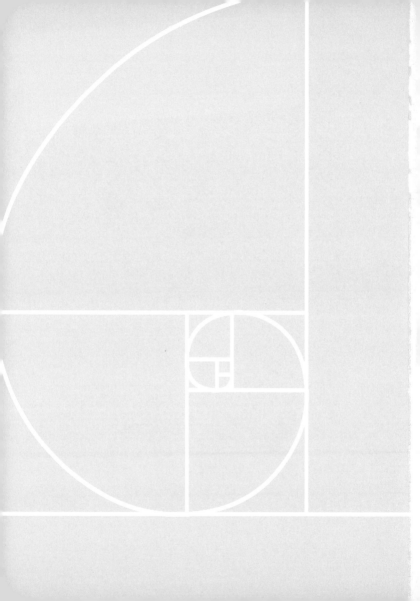

LLEWELLYN'S
Little Book of
NUMEROLOGY

© Jason Fell Photography

Richard Webster (New Zealand) is the bestselling author of more than one hundred books. Richard has appeared on several radio and television programs in the US and abroad, including guest spots on WMAQ-TV (Chicago), KTLA-TV (Los Angeles), and KSTW-TV (Seattle). He travels regularly, lecturing and conducting workshops on a variety of metaphysical subjects. His bestselling titles include *Spirit Guides & Angel Guardians* and *Creative Visualization for Beginners*. Learn more at Psychic.co.nz.

LLEWELLYN'S
Little Book of
NUMEROLOGY

RICHARD WEBSTER

LLEWELLYN
WOODBURY, MINNESOTA

FIRST EDITION
First Printing, 2025

Cover cartouche by Freepik
Cover design by Shira Atakpu
Interior art by Llewellyn Art Department

Llewellyn Publications is a registered trademark of Llewellyn Worldwide Ltd.

Library of Congress Cataloging-in-Publication Data Pending
ISBN: 978-0-7387-7842-6

Llewellyn Publications
A Division of Llewellyn Worldwide Ltd.
2143 Wooddale Drive
Woodbury, MN 55125-2989
www.llewellyn.com

Printed in China

MIX
Paper | Supporting
responsible forestry
FSC® C144853

For my good friend, Mick Peck

Contents

Exercise List

INTRODUCTION

Numerology is a metaphysical system that studies the mystical significance of numbers and their influence on human life. At times, we've all wondered if we're following the right path in life. Numerology is a wonderful tool to confirm that you are on track and, if you aren't, help you find the right one. The happiest people are the ones doing what they're meant to be doing in this lifetime. You'll be able to discover talents that you didn't know you possessed and even work out the best times to move house, change jobs, or seek a new relationship.

You'll also be able to interpret other important numbers such as your age, house number, graduation date, date of marriage, date you started working at your current job, and other memorable dates and numbers in your life. You might like to check out nicknames or compare the different vibrations created by signing your name using initials and surname compared to your first and last names, for instance. If your name happens to be Susanna but everyone knows you as Sue, Suze, or Suzie, you can find out which works better for you.

Numerology can help you choose the right career, make important decisions, and plan your future. Numerology helps you relate better with others, too. You can use it to determine your compatibility with a friend, work colleague, or potential partner.

Our lives revolve around numbers. In his 2014 book, *Our Mathematical Universe*, MIT professor Max Tegmark investigates the possibility that numbers not only describe the universe, but actually make the universe. In our own lives, numbers are used in almost everything we do. You use numbers every time you call someone on your phone, use an elevator, make appointments, or check the time. You decide whether to buy something by comparing prices. If you're working on losing weight, numbers can motivate you. You can't draw up a budget, determine profit or loss, or check your grocery bill without using numbers. Numbers record your age, the length of your relationships, and the number of times you've watched a favorite movie. They also keep track of your bank balance and let you know how well your favorite team is doing. You can't even visit someone without knowing the number in their address.

Most people have a favorite number. Both Beyoncé and her husband Jay-Z are extreme examples. They love the number 4. This may be because Beyoncé was born on September 4, Jay-Z was born on December 4, and they married each other on April 4 (4/4). They love the number so much that they got matching *IV* finger tattoos to commemorate their wedding in 2008.

The purpose of this book is to help you realize the significant role numbers play in everyone's lives. By the time you've finished reading it, you'll know much more about the personalities, talents, strengths, weaknesses, and future trends of all the people you interact with. You'll also have a much deeper understanding of yourself, and a clear sense of where you're going in this lifetime.

Chapter One

THE NUMBERS
OF NUMEROLOGY

There are eleven numbers in numerology: 1, 2, 3, 4, 5, 6, 7, 8, 9, 11, and 22. 11 and 22 are called master numbers and rarely get reduced to a single digit. Each number relates to a different aspect of life and can be thought of as a lesson that should be learned in this lifetime.

The numbers can be used positively or negatively, and consequently reveal people's strengths and weaknesses, depending on how they are used.

Each number also has a number of correspondences, such as colors, crystals, and herbs which can be used to increase the effectiveness of the number's energy.

Number 1

COLOR: Red
GEMSTONE: Ruby
HERBS: Basil, woodruff
PLANET: Sun

This has always been considered a harmonious, prosperous, and lucky number. It is considered the father of all numbers. In the tarot, number one is represented by the Magician, who is ambitious, strong, in control, and has the potential to manifest anything.

Number 1 represents individuality, independence, attainment, and new beginnings. It's associated with ambition, leadership, confidence, courage, assertiveness, action, innovation, creativity, originality, and power. People with a one in their chart like to stand on their own two feet and lead the way forward.

Number 2

COLORS: Orange, white
GEMSTONES: Pearl, moonstone

HERBS: Anise, orris

PLANET: Moon

This number is traditionally thought to be related to the intellect and is considered the mother of all numbers. It symbolizes duality, and the two opposites that cannot live without each other, such as night and day, male and female, tall and short, and yin and yang.

Number 2 is associated with cooperation, balance, duality, and harmony. It is related to partnerships, collaboration, adaptability, charm, sensitivity, tactfulness, understanding, and diplomacy. People with a 2 in their chart are often the power behind the throne, as they are supportive, tender-hearted, natural peacemakers who achieve their goals without confrontation.

Number 3

COLOR: Yellow

GEMSTONE: Yellow sapphire

HERBS: Fennel, lavender

PLANET: Jupiter

This number is traditionally considered holy; it's the number of the father, son, and holy spirit of Christianity as well as the trinity of father, mother, and child. Three symbolizes fertility, abundance, and fruitfulness.

Number 3 represents communication, creativity, and self-expression. It is related to joy, optimism, and social activities. People with a 3 in their chart are easygoing, fun-loving, good-natured, and popular. Because they are artistic and have good imaginations, they often work in creative fields.

Number 4

COLOR: Green
GEMSTONES: Turquoise, lapis lazuli
HERBS: Comfrey, mullein
PLANET: Uranus

Pythagoras, the father of numerology, regarded this as the foundation of all the other numbers. It's square in shape, which makes it the number of solidity, endurance, will-power, and firmness of purpose.

Number 4 represents stability, practicality, and hard work. It is related to reliability, dependability, discipline, punctuality, attention to detail, focus, and slow but steady progress. People with a 4 in their chart are conventional, cautious, loyal, practical, well-organized, and hard-working.

The
four most
important numbers
in your chart reveal your
purpose in life, opportunities,
your abilities, and your motivation. They're all potentials, and it's up
to you what you do with them. Every
number can be used positively or negatively, and most of us reflect both positive
and negative qualities at different times and in
different situations.

Number 5

COLOR: Blue
GEMSTONE: Blue opal
HERBS: Damiana, dragon's blood
PLANET: Mercury

Traditionally, this was considered a magical number, and the five-pointed pentacle has been used as a powerful and protective amulet for thousands of years. Five was also related to justice and faith. The Hierophant is the fifth card in the major arcana of the Tarot.

Number 5 represents change, variety, adaptability, versatility, and freedom. It is related to curiosity, adventure, travel, playfulness, and new experiences. People with a 5 in their charts are spontaneous, flexible, enthusiastic, and need plenty of stimulation as they get bored easily.

Number 6

COLOR: Indigo
GEMSTONE: Sapphire
HERBS: Boneset, catnip
PLANET: Venus

Traditionally, this number was considered sacred to Venus. Not surprisingly, the sixth card in the major arcana of the tarot deck is the Lovers. The Bible says that the world was made in six days; as six was also the day humans were created, it was at one time called the number of humanity.

Number 6 represents love, romance, harmony, nurture, and home and family responsibilities. It is related to relationships, compassion, kindness, and creativity. People with a 6 in their chart are affectionate, generous, kind, forgiving, responsible, community-minded, and frequently artistic.

Number 7

COLOR: Violet

GEMSTONES: Amethyst, purple sapphire

HERBS: Mugwort, poppy

PLANET: Neptune

The ancient Pythagoreans called this number the vehicle of humanity: there were seven days, planets, metals, and even ages of man. Because of this, the number was considered especially lucky. It was also the number of perfection, as the sum of the holy number three and the four traditional elements adds up to seven. This number was also a symbol of eternal life to ancient Egyptians.

Number 7 represents introspection, spirituality, philosophy, knowledge, and inner wisdom. It is related to intellectual pursuits, understanding, intuition, and spiritual growth. People with a 7 in their chart are analytical, technical, refined, reserved, and patient.

Number 8

COLORS: Brown, green
GEMSTONE: Quartz
HERBS: Hyssop, lovage
PLANET: Saturn

This number was traditionally known as the number of justice. Many tarot decks, including the Marseilles Tarot, have Justice as the eighth card in the major arcana. However, in 1909 Arthur Edward Waite swapped the positions of the eighth and eleventh cards to make Strength the eighth card and Justice the eleventh in the Rider-Waite-Smith deck. Most modern tarot decks have followed suit.

Number 8 represents material success, abundance, and achievement. It is related to power, achievement, status, and financial and career growth. People with an 8 in their chart are loyal, strong willed, responsible, hard-working, and goal oriented.

Number 9

COLOR: Rose
GEMSTONES: Diamond, rose quartz
HERB: Cinnamon, clove
PLANET: Mars

Ancient priests used this number to help cure illnesses. It was considered a number of power, wisdom, and protection. As it was the sum of three multiplied by itself, nine was associated with intellectual and spiritual knowledge.

Number 9 is associated with humanitarianism, compassion, completion, and spiritual awareness. It relates to idealism, selflessness, universal love, and giving to others. People with a 9 in their chart are broad-minded, inspirational, philosophical, tolerant, and artistic.

The Master Numbers

Master numbers provide the people who have them with increased capabilities but at a high price, including a degree of nervous tension that is rarely hidden from others.

Number Eleven

COLOR: Silver
GEMSTONE: Diamond

HERBS: Chamomile, rosemary

PLANET: Sun

This number is linked to intuition, insight, inspiration, dreams, enlightenment, higher consciousness, and spiritual awareness. People with an 11 in their chart usually have a strong intuition, a deep level of understanding, and powerful empathy. People with master numbers in their makeup are usually late bloomers, as it takes them many years to be able to make good use of the added potentials that the master number brings.

Number Twenty-Two

COLOR: Gold

GEMSTONE: Coral

HERB: Fly agaric

PLANET: Earth

The other master number in numerology, 22 is often known as the Master Builder, as people who have this number in their chart have the potential to turn their dreams into reality. People with a 22 as a major number in their chart possess the ability to achieve on a large scale. They are practical and have the potential to manifest whatever it is they desire. Like the 11, people with a 22 in their chart are usually late bloomers. Number 22 has always been considered an especially important number. There are, for instance, 22 letters in the Hebrew alphabet, 22 pathways in the Kabbalah, and 22 major arcana cards in the standard tarot deck.

. . .

The numbers are all connected to each other in a variety of ways. Each number is a logical step forward from the previous number. For example, the material desires of 8 are followed by the generosity and selflessness of 9. The self-centeredness and independence of 1 is followed by the cooperation and harmony of 2.

The odd numbers relate to the individual, while even numbers deal with practical concerns.

Some numbers work well with each other, as they share similar traits and desires. Numbers 3, 6, and 9, for instance, all have creative potential. The numbers 2, 6, and 9 are all involved in cooperating and helping others. Last, 1, 4, and 8 are all willing to work hard and enjoy achieving practical and financial goals.

The Negative Side of the Numbers

Although it would be wonderful if everyone worked solely with the positive traits their numbers provided, this is impossible, as even the most optimistic and positive thinkers have low periods from time to time. To provide balance, here are the negative traits of each number.

Number One

KEYWORDS: Self, dependence

On the negative path, ones can often appear to be subjugated and codependent. They need to overcome this dependence before they can start becoming independent. Some number ones think solely of themselves and have little interest in the desires and needs of others. These people are highly self-centered and egotistical; usually they're covering up an inferiority complex.

Number Two

KEYWORD: Sensitivity

Negative twos can be overly shy, self-effacing, and pessimistic. They often seem apathetic. Sometimes negative twos will fight against the role they've been given and try to become leaders but it seldom works, and they usually blame others for their own lack of success.

Number Three

KEYWORD: Superficiality

Negative threes often waste time and fritter their energies away. They're likely to dabble in many areas, scattering their forces in too many directions. All threes should be aware that they can slip into superficial and frivolous lives all too easily.

Number Four

KEYWORD: Drudgery

Negative fours are so tied down with feelings of limitation and frustration that they frequently find themselves in ruts of their own making. Their rigidity and stubbornness make it hard for them to realize that they're the architects of their own misfortune.

Number Five

KEYWORD: Self-indulgence

Negative fives find it hard to stick at any one thing, as they are surrounded by opportunities on all sides. They often get lost in self-indulgence, especially in gratifying their sensual desires.

Number Six
KEYWORD: Critic

Fortunately, there are very few negative sixes. Occasionally, some become overwhelmed with responsibility and find themselves being misused and taken advantage of by others. Some negative sixes are overly critical and meddle in other people's business.

Number Seven
KEYWORD: Introspection

Negative sevens can be so withdrawn and self-centered that they retreat from almost every situation. They're also nervous, which makes it hard for them to relate well with others. Their self-imposed isolation hinders their growth and development in this incarnation.

Number Eight
KEYWORD: Demander

Negative eights can misuse their power and become tyrants. Because they're impatient, they often fail to achieve their desires. Even when they succeed, they derive little pleasure from their accomplishments.

Number Nine
KEYWORD: Egotist

Many negative nines are aimless dreamers, living more in their minds than in the real world. Some are ambitious and unwilling to accept the selflessness that is vital for their development. When they fail to find their right path, they become frustrated and bitter.

Number Eleven
KEYWORD: Fanatic

Negative elevens are aware of their special capabilities but use them to satisfy their own selfish desires. They may have delusions of grandeur and want everything to be done their way.

Number Twenty-Two
KEYWORD: Greed

Negative twenty-twos are total materialists and will do anything to achieve their goals. They often succeed but are seldom satisfied—deep down, they know that they're not achieving their purpose in this lifetime.

Your Most Important Numbers

The most important numbers in a numerology chart are:

- The life path, derived from the numbers in the person's full date of birth
- The expression, which comes from all the letters in a person's full name at birth converted into numbers
- The soul urge, which comes from all the vowels in the person's full name at birth converted into numbers
- The birthday, from the person's birth month and day

The life path is the most important of these and represents approximately 40 percent of the person's makeup. The expression is about 30 percent, the soul urge about 20, and the day number about 10. There is much more to numerology than these four numbers, but we're covering the relative importance of each main number.

In numerology it is generally thought that if we were born on a particular date and given the correct full name at birth, we will experience a particular set of numbers that will give us the best opportunity to progress in this incarnation.

In the next chapter we'll look at the life path, which reveals the person's purpose in this lifetime.

Chapter Two

THE LIFE PATH NUMBER

The most important number in a numerology chart is the life path number. It's so significant that it's sometimes referred to as the person's destiny number. Unlike some of the other numbers in a numerology chart, it cannot change—it is based on the month, day, and year of birth.

Your life path number reveals your purpose in this lifetime and consequently shows what you should be doing with your life. Many people fight against this number, as they don't like the particular destiny that their number reveals, but it never works—deep down, they're aware that they aren't doing what they're meant to be doing with their lives. Someone with a 2 life path might desire to be a leader. This person might achieve that goal but will never be a great leader, as their destiny is to be the power behind the throne. Should the person accept this, they have the potential to be a huge success in that role, as it is what they were born to do. Likewise, someone with a 9 life path might want to make a great deal of money but doing so will never provide any long-term satisfaction, as they will be ignoring what they're here for, which is to help humanity. However, people on a 9 life path *can* make money as a result of their creativity or service to others.

· · · Exercise One · · ·
How to Determine Your Life Path Number

Your life path number is determined by reducing your date of birth to a single digit, or possibly one of the master numbers 11 or 22. The best way to work out your life path is by listing your month, day, and year of birth in the form of a sum, as important numbers can be lost if the numbers are added up in a straight line.

Your most important number is your life path number, which is derived from your full date of birth. Someone with a life path of 3 is friendly, sociable, and positive. They make friends easily, are good conversationalists, and are fun to be with. People with this life path number have a good imagination and would do well in a creative field that uses communication skills. They have good taste and enjoy beauty in all its forms. They are adaptable, versatile, and curious but sometimes move too rapidly from one interest to another. Their purpose in this lifetime is to learn to express themselves and inspire others with their creativity and communication skills.

Here's an example of someone born on December 28, 1989:

$$12 + 28 + 1989 = 2029$$
$$2 + 0 + 2 + 9 = 13$$
$$1 + 3 = 4$$

This person's life path number is 4.

Here's an example of someone born on November 29, 1996:

$$11 + 29 + 1996 = 2036$$
$$2 + 0 + 3 + 6 = 11$$

As 11 is a master number, it is not reduced.

This next example is of someone born on February 29, 1944. It shows how an important number can be lost if the calculation is not done correctly:

$$2 + 29 + 1944 = 1975$$
$$1 + 9 + 7 + 5 = 22$$

If this person's numbers had been added up in a straight line and then reduced, we would have ended up with an incorrect Life Path number: $2 + 2 + 9 + 1 + 9 + 4 + 4 = 31$. Reducing further to $3 + 1 = 4$, rendering the master number lost.

What the Life Path Reveals

There are eleven possible life paths: 1 to 9, plus the master numbers 11 and 22. The life path cannot precisely specify the career a person should pursue, as it is modified by all the other numbers in a numerology chart. In fact, most people have many conflicting numbers in their charts, to complicate matters. Consequently, although some are fortunate enough to know exactly what they want to do with their lives at an early age, most people gradually find out what it is at some stage during their lives. And of course, some people never work out what they should be doing.

You can picture your life path as a huge, limitless circle of energy with yourself placed in the center, from which there are myriad paths in every direction. You can travel anywhere you wish within your life path circle and therefore have a virtually unlimited amount of freedom in what you do. All the opportunities and experiences you need to work with in this lifetime are there waiting for you. People who work inside their life path circle have the potential to find happiness and success in this incarnation.

However, some people leave their circle when they look around and see what the other ten life path circles have to offer. Another circle may appear easier or more stimulating. It's easy to move to another circle because everything is connected and the eleven life paths appear in the form of a hologram. The people who move to another circle may be lucky enough to find a degree of success there but won't ever feel truly satisfied, as they're not doing what they're supposed to be doing in this lifetime.

Every life path contains both challenges and opportunities. The people who achieve the greatest success work on overcoming challenges and take advantage of the opportunities.

Life Path 1

KEYWORDS: Independence, ambition, motivation

People on a 1 life path often start out in life by being dependent and needing to learn independence. It takes most 1s a great deal of time and effort to accomplish this. Once they've done that, they can harness their skills and use their drive, motivation, originality, inner strength, and independence to achieve their goals. They possess a great deal of drive and energy and are happiest when working toward worthwhile, positive goals. Even when they don't seek the position, they often find themselves in a leadership role. Their potential for success and accomplishment is usually obvious to others, though they themselves may not be aware of it, especially early on in life. Once on track, they enjoy achieving their goals and receiving recognition from others.

People on a 1 life path have a practical, logical approach to problems and can convince others that their solution is the right one. They are natural salespeople and generally do well in business. There's a strong need for them to demonstrate their individuality and personal power. There's also a degree of self-centeredness in all people on this life path, though many have learned how to disguise it, if only partially.

The life purpose of people on a 1 life path is to stand on their own two feet and achieve independence. Their ultimate goal is to become a leader.

Children on a 1 life path are independent, know their own minds, and like to do things their own way. They often assume leadership roles when playing with other children. They have good ideas and original approaches. However, they want to get their own way and usually need to learn that other people have good ideas, too.

Challenges

The most important challenge for people on a 1 life path is to develop self-confidence and to start believing in themselves. Self-doubt is a common challenge for many young people on this life path, but it is usually overcome by the time they reach their mid-twenties. Many people on this life path find it difficult to find a balance between their own personal ambitions and considering the needs of others.

Opportunities

People on a 1 life path have the potential to become leaders in their chosen fields. If they're ambitious, stand on their own two feet, seize opportunities, and work hard, they can achieve all the success they desire.

Life Path 2

KEYWORDS: Sensitive, diplomatic, cooperative

People on a 2 life path are friendly, considerate, and tactful people who are sensitive to the feelings and moods of others. They are good organizers and often choose careers that involve helping others. They're usually content to stay in the background and seldom receive full credit for their contributions. Early on in life, people on a 2 life path can be overly sensitive and may need to learn how to handle things so that they aren't constantly hurt by others. On the whole, 2 life path people are easy to get along with and work well with others. They work best when they can work at their own pace and feel unsettled and insecure when pushed or pressured too much. People on this life path are natural peacemakers who have a talent for soothing other people's feelings. They love their friends and receive a great deal of love in return. They can be indecisive and find it hard to make decisions. They tend to be overgenerous, a trait that other people can take advantage of. Being the number of a traditional couple, they are happiest inside a permanent relationship and dislike living on their own.

The life purpose of people on a 2 life path is to develop their skills at working with others to provide comfort, guidance, protection, and support.

Children on a 2 life path are sensitive and feel things deeply. Because of this, they quickly learn to keep many of their thoughts private to avoid possible ridicule or rejection. They are often creative but can be reticent in showing their work because their sensitive natures are finely tuned when it comes to rejection. Children on a 2 life path thrive on encouragement from their parents and significant role models.

Challenges

People on a 2 life path frequently have challenges relating to assertiveness and self-expression that is usually expressed as indecisiveness, passiveness, avoiding confrontation, co-dependence, and putting other people's needs before their own. Some of these challenges can be overcome quickly, but others can take many years to overcome.

Opportunities

People on a 2 life path work well in partnerships as well as caring and supportive environments. As they go through life, they'll have plenty of opportunities to develop their empathy, diplomatic skills, nurturing qualities, and strong intuition. Should they develop these skills healthily, they'll have fulfilling and loving relationships as well as a strong, close family life.

Life Path 3

KEYWORDS: Creativity, self-expression, communication

People on a 3 life path are friendly, sociable, positive, enthusiastic, and outgoing. They're good conversationalists and are constantly full of original ideas that they express in an entertaining way. They make friends easily; they're open, affectionate, warm, and fun to be with. They find it easy to communicate with others. They also have excellent imaginations, which can often lead to careers in a creative field, usually one that involves their communication skills. They have good taste and enjoy beauty in all its forms. Many people on this life path are highly talented but fail to take their skills as far as they could. They often give up something they're naturally good at to pursue something that seems easier or appears more lucrative. They have keen, curious minds and learn quickly.

They're adaptable and move rapidly from one interest to another. Some become dilettantes and fail to learn much about any one topic, preferring to dabble in a variety of different activities, but it can lead to frustration.

The life purpose of people on a 3 life path is to learn to express themselves and inspire others with their creativity and communication skills.

Children on a 3 life path are creative and imaginative. They have plenty of energy and enjoy getting involved in every activity that appeals to them. They get on well with others and make friends everywhere they go. At some stage during their childhood, they need to learn that a less scattered and more disciplined approach produces better results.

Challenges

People on a 3 life path find it easy to scatter their energy. Consequently, their greatest challenge is to stay focused and use their communication skills wisely. Many 3s fail to make good use of their creative talents. Self-doubt, impatience, and lack of self-discipline are also challenges for many on this life path.

Opportunities

People on a 3 life path are blessed with significant creative potential and receive many opportunities to express themselves creatively. They usually have a talent with words and many work in careers that involve communication or the arts. They have the potential to inspire and motivate others with their enthusiasm and vivaciousness.

Life Path 4

KEYWORDS: Practicality, dependability, hard-working

People on a 4 life path are prepared to work hard to achieve their goals. They're conscientious, serious, loyal, patient, stable, responsible, and determined. They make good managers and organizers, and they enjoy dealing with large-scale projects. People on this life path make few mistakes—they're methodical, take their time, pay attention to details, and work everything out before acting. They can create order out of chaos and like to finish what they start. They enjoy routine and organization but sometimes feel hemmed in or restricted, so it's important for them to learn how to work within the limits they find.

The life purpose of people on a 4 life path is to accept the limitations they experience and to do the best work they can within these boundaries. Their task is to bring stability, order, organization, and patience to everything they do.

Virtually from birth, children on a 4 life path approach life in a practical, clear, down-to-earth way. They are serious, logical, sincere, and honest. They are persuasive and express themselves well. Their main fault is stubbornness and rigidity, which holds them back until they learn to be more easygoing. It's important for them to realize that their way of doing something is not the only way. Life becomes easier once they learn how to cooperate and work with others.

Challenges

Stubbornness and rigidity are the major challenges for most people on a 4 life path. They dislike change and can be overly cautious and risk-averse. Because they find it hard to adapt to change, they frequently refuse to investigate new ideas.

Opportunities

People on a 4 life path are well-organized and practical, and they pay attention to detail. They're hard-working and persistent. They work and live in the material world and have the potential to use their skills to build a strong foundation and achieve financial success.

Life Path 5

KEYWORDS: Adventurous, versatile, freedom-loving

People on a 5 life path love change, variety, and adventure. They're versatile, resourceful, enthusiastic, curious, capable, and quick-thinking. They seem to remain forever young, as there are always many exciting opportunities to explore. They love freedom but often need to learn how to use their time wisely and productively. Travel often plays an important role in their lives, and they feel at home everywhere they go. Their restlessness means it can take many years for these people to find the right opportunity for them. They have a genuine interest in others. They're independent in both thought and action, so it's easy for them to feel stifled in routine occupations. They're always looking ahead, seeking experiences and opportunities.

The life purpose of people on a 5 life path is to learn from experience, to make good use of their time, and to achieve worthwhile goals.

Children on a 5 life path love excitement, stimulation, change, and new activities. They are talented, resourceful, and curious. They're enthusiastic about trying anything new and appealing. Unfortunately, they get bored easily and become agitated and impatient when faced with every-day humdrum tasks. Life becomes easier as they grow and learn to focus their attention on one thing at a time.

Challenges

The main challenge for people on a 5 life path is to use their time wisely. They need constant stimulation and find exciting opportunities everywhere. Consequently, they're inclined to move on to the next activity before they've finished the previous one. Restlessness and impulsiveness can also cause problems. Their strong desire for freedom makes it hard for them to commit to anything long term.

Opportunities

People on this life path see opportunities and adventure everywhere, and it often takes them many years before they settle down and make positive use of their versatility and love of change. They have the potential to motivate and inspire others with their enthusiasm and adventurous nature.

Life Path 6

KEYWORDS: Family, responsibility, love

People on a 6 life path are honest, sincere, sympathetic, and caring. They enjoy home and family life. They're always willing to help others and accept responsibility readily, which often makes them the person in the family to whom people come when they need help or want someone to take charge. People on this life path appreciate beauty in all its forms and usually have an artistic side to their nature. They are generous in every sense of the word and enjoy sharing what they have with others. They often find themselves in positions of trust and take these responsibilities seriously. They are happiest inside a stable, loving, long-term relationship.

The life purpose of people on a 6 life path is to learn to express their innate love, compassion, and desire to serve and help others.

Children on a 6 life path are usually kind, sympathetic, and loving. They want to please others and enjoy helping with everyday household chores. They are compassionate and quick to sense the feelings of adults, children, and even animals. They can be overly willing to please and give way to others rather than express their own personal wants and needs.

Challenges

The main challenge for people on a 6 life path is to balance their own needs with those of others. They may also have difficulty with responsibility, a need for perfection, and the tendency to be self-sacrificing. Worrying can also be a major concern. People on this life path sometimes become complacent and fail to achieve all they can in life.

Opportunities

People on this path are drawn to helping others. This often leads to a career involving their nurturing and healing skills. They find satisfaction and fulfilment in long-term as well as loving relationships, and they enjoy serving their communities in ways both small and large.

Life Path 7

KEYWORDS: Analytical, introspective, philosophical

People on a 7 life path like to do things in their own way and usually show little interest in other solutions. They are reserved, so it takes time for people to get to know them well. They are deep thinkers who like peace and quiet, and they need plenty of time to grow spiritually and intuitively. They seek the truth and can be outspoken and blunt when they see anything they don't approve of. People on this life path have analytical minds and can often be found working in technical fields, such as computer programming.

The life purpose of people on a 7 life path is to learn and understand life's deeper meaning.

Children on a 7 life path are usually quiet and keep most of their thoughts to themselves. They find it hard to trust others and prefer to rely on themselves. They are intelligent and enjoy learning, especially about topics that are involved and complex. They become less reserved and more communicative as they get older.

Challenges

People on a 7 life path need to learn how to balance their analytical ability with their spiritual perceptions. They have a slightly different approach, which other people may misinterpret as aloofness or a sense of superiority, that can lead to loneliness. It's important for them to play a part in the world rather than spending all their time in solitary pursuits.

Opportunities

People on this life path enjoy researching, studying, and analyzing anything that interests them. Consequently, many people on this life path can be found working in education, science, or a career they find mentally stimulating and challenging. Their unique perceptions give them the opportunity to make significant contributions to whatever field they choose to work in. Although many try to fight it, spirituality always plays a major role in their lives, whether as a believer or a skeptic.

Life Path 8

KEYWORDS: Ambition, material success, leadership

People on an 8 life path are confident, ambitious, courageous, forceful, dependable, reliable, and practical. They have leadership skills and can motivate and direct others. They are goal-oriented and work hard to achieve their financial goals. They enjoy setting and achieving goals and then moving on to something more challenging. People on this life path are inclined to be stubborn and find it hard to accept other people's advice and suggestions. Success and status are important to them. Once they've achieved their financial goals, some people on this life path show that they've learned this lesson by using their skills and resources to help people who are less fortunate.

The life purpose of people on an 8 life path is to learn to understand and deal with the material world in an ethical manner.

Children on an 8 life path are responsible, reliable, practical, and ambitious. They know what they want and become stubborn when their desires are thwarted. They are interested in money and learn how to handle it at a young age. They become more adaptable and gain people skills as they mature.

Challenges

People on an 8 life path usually have challenges relating to power and financial success. These issues can be caused by materialism, a tendency to overwork, or misuse of power and money. They tend to value everything in financial terms—the more expensive something is, the more they appreciate it. Sometimes they even judge their friends by how financially successful they are. Life becomes easier for them when they learn to balance their strong inner drive with integrity and allow sufficient time for a mutually satisfying home and family life.

Opportunities

People on this life path have the potential to become leaders and to achieve financial success. If they keep high ethical standards, they can use their drive and abilities to achieve significant success and help many others in the process.

Life Path 9

KEYWORDS: Compassion, idealism, humanitarianism

People on a 9 life path are idealistic, compassionate, considerate, kind, loving, and tolerant. They have a giving nature that often comes at great personal expense to themselves. Their greatest satisfaction is derived from helping and giving to others. They are also sensitive and easily hurt by others' comments and actions. This sensitivity often finds expression in some form of creativity. Their greatest opportunities for success come from their appreciation of, and often considerable talent in, the creative arts.

The life purpose of people on a 9 life path is to use their creativity, humanitarianism, compassion, and love to make the world a better place for everyone.

Children on a 9 life path are affectionate, kind, and sympathetic. They're sensitive to other people's needs and enjoy helping them. They are often creative, and as long as they receive encouragement from friends and family, they can take these skills a long way.

Challenges

People on a 9 life path often need to learn forgiveness, as they have a tendency to hold on to hurts and grievances. Learning to let go of the past can prove difficult. They may resent the fact that they appear to be endlessly giving to others without receiving much in return. Life becomes easier once they realize that their joys come through the act of giving. They need to remain aware of the influence they have on others and provide a good example by living up to the ideals they express.

Opportunities

People on this life path are deeply compassionate and have the potential to make a difference in the world with their love, spirituality, and humanitarianism. They also have the potential to give to others through some form of creativity.

Life Path 11

KEYWORDS: Visionary, spirituality, inspiration

People on an 11 life path are extremely capable at everything they do, as they possess the additional insights and perception that this master number gives them. However, they are also idealistic dreamers, which means they often think about the great things they're going to accomplish but never quite manage to achieve. They possess considerable spiritual and intuitive capabilities, which can be hard to handle while they're young. There is always a degree of nervous tension associated with all master numbers, and the awareness and sensitivity that people on this life path experience can be extremely hard to handle. Some 11s find this life path too difficult to handle and prefer to live as 2s, even though they subconsciously know that this level does not offer what they're here to learn. People on an 11 life path are often considered old souls, which means they have learned the easier lessons in previous lifetimes and must now experience the life of a master number.

The life purpose of people on an 11 life path is to inspire others with their insights and perceptions.

Children on an 11 life path are extremely sensitive and easily hurt. They are naturally intuitive and spiritual. They spend a great deal of time daydreaming, as they usually prefer their own inner worlds to the more risky and sometimes harsh outer world. They tend to be naive and vulnerable in their early years but gain strength and a sense of purpose as they mature.

Challenges

People on an 11 life path have a number of challenges that need to be overcome before they can make full use of their significant potential. Because they're extremely sensitive, their emotions overwhelm them at times. They're also easily affected by the emotions of others. They usually suffer from self-doubt and anxiety that can affect their confidence. They live in a world of thoughts and therefore usually lack practicality, which can cause problems with routine tasks.

Opportunities

People on this master number life path have the potential to develop their spiritual and intuitive natures and ultimately become a source of help and inspiration to others. Elevens are often charismatic and can use this talent to create positive change in the world. They can develop their artistic side to create works that inspire others.

Life Path 22

KEYWORDS: Master builder, sometimes also master teacher and master architect

People on a 22 life path are extremely capable at everything they do and often rise to the top in whatever career they choose. Some find work that benefits humanity on a national or international level. Even when they're not making use of their full potential, it is obvious to others. They operate on a different level from most people, which gives them access to unique solutions that they can turn to their advantage. People on this life path are practical but frequently adopt an unconventional approach that makes them seem unusual or strange. Because of the degree of nervous tension that surrounds them, many people on this life path are frustrated, and only a few achieve more than a small part of their potential in this incarnation. Like those on an 11 life path, people on this life path are considered old souls. And like their 11 life path counterparts living at the 2 level, 22s can operate at a 4 level if they find the pressures of a master number too difficult.

The life purpose of people on a 22 life path is to use their considerable skills and understanding to benefit humanity as a whole. It usually takes 22s many incarnations to fulfil this goal.

Children on a 22 life path love to learn but can be easily distracted with the wealth of opportunities they see everywhere. Their superior skills are obvious at an early age, but they usually need careful parental guidance; not all of their many ideas are realistic and practical. Their early potential will be obvious to everyone, but they are unlikely to show more than great promise during childhood given the amount of time it takes most 22s to get on track.

Challenges

People on a 22 life path set high standards for themselves and become frustrated when the results are less than perfect. They have a strong desire to improve the world in some way, which causes problems when they must balance their idealism against the realities of the situation. Coupled with their nervous tension and powerful emotions, the weight of the responsibility they carry regularly creates challenges.

Opportunities

People on this life path are able to turn their dreams into reality. They are well-organized and willing to work hard and long to achieve their goals, and they enjoy solving problems. They make good leaders and often possess strong entrepreneurial capabilities. If they use these skills to benefit humanity, they have the potential to achieve greatness.

In the next chapter we'll look at the second of the most important four numbers in your chart: your expression number.

Chapter Three
THE EXPRESSION NUMBER

The expression number reveals people's natural abilities. Everyone is born with a selection of talents, skills, and potentials, and the expression number tells the world what these are. It reveals the person's general direction in life and is the number that is most often recognized by others, as it clearly reveals the characteristics that make each person who they are. In contrast to this, the characteristics of the life path number are often concealed, especially if the person is struggling to learn the lessons that they are here to learn.

The expression number is helpful in determining potential careers, as people are always happiest in an occupation that makes use of their natural talents and abilities.

• • • Exercise Two • • •

How to Determine Your Expression Number

Your expression number is derived by turning all the letters in your full name at birth into numbers, and then reducing them down to a single digit (or the master numbers, 11 or 22) using this chart (applicable to the rest of the book):

1	2	3	4	5	6	7	8	9
A	B	C	D	E	F	G	H	I
J	K	L	M	N	O	P	Q	R
S	T	U	V	W	X	Y	Z	

Here is an example for someone named Suzanne Kay Roberts:

SUZANNE

$$1 + 3 + 8 + 1 + 5 + 5 + 5 = 28$$

$$2 + 8 = 10$$

$$1 + 0 = 1$$

KAY

$$2 + 1 + 7 = 10$$

$$1 + 0 = 1$$

ROBERTS

$$9 + 6 + 2 + 5 + 9 + 2 + 1 = 34$$

$$3 + 4 = 7$$

Add the three numbers from all three names:

$$1 + 1 + 7 = 9$$

Suzanne's expression number is 9. It's important to total and reduce each individual name separately. If you add all the numbers in the person's name at once, you may miss a master number or receive one that doesn't apply.

It's possible to find master numbers (11 and 22) in individual names; these are not reduced until the final stage of working out the expression number. Elvis Presley is a striking example of this:

ELVIS

$$5 + 3 + 4 + 9 + 1 = 22$$

AARON

$$1 + 1 + 9 + 6 + 5 = 22$$

PRESLEY

$$7 + 9 + 5 + 1 + 3 + 5 + 7 = 37$$

$$3 + 7 = 10$$

$$1 + 0 = 1$$

Add the three numbers:

$$22 + 22 + 1 = 45$$

$$4 + 5 = 9$$

Nine is his expression number

If all the numbers in Elvis's three names had been added up together, the two master numbers would have been lost. It's important to preserve these, as each part of the full name provides information about a person's natural abilities. The number of the first or given name reveals something of the person's feelings. The second name reveals latent potential, and the third or surname provides clues to the person's family background.

What the Expression Number Reveals

People with a 1 expression possess leadership potential and a strong desire to demonstrate their worth. They're ambitious, determined, and independent. They have an original approach to everything they do. They prefer dealing with

Your expression number reveals your natural abilities. It is derived by turning all the letters in your full name at birth into numbers and then reducing the total of these to a single digit or master number. People with an expression number of 1 have leadership potential, and a strong desire to demonstrate their ability. They're ambitious, determined, and independent. They have an original approach to everything they do.

immediate situations rather than planning and organizing long-term projects. They enjoy working for themselves or may choose to climb up the ranks in a larger organization until they've gained a position of seniority and responsibility. People who use their 1 expression number negatively can be aggressive, stubborn, and selfish, or self-conscious, lazy, and dependent.

People with a 2 expression relate well with others. They're friendly, cooperative, diplomatic, and sensitive to other people's moods and feelings. They make good mediators—they're supportive, kind, and tactful. They're easy to get on with, and achieve their goals with quiet, gentle persuasion. They enjoy making plans but prefer other people to execute them. People who use their 2 expression number negatively are easily hurt, indecisive, insecure, spiteful, and apathetic.

People with a 3 expression are enthusiastic, cheerful, positive, and optimistic. They are confident people who are naturally good at some form of self-expression, such as talking, writing, and singing. People who use their 3 expression negatively are superficial, overly sensitive, vain, impatient, and gossipy.

People with a 4 expression have a practical, down-to-earth approach to everything they do. They're conscientious, reliable, and patient. They work well within the limits placed on them and make good managers and planners. They're often attracted to careers in scientific and mechanical fields. People who use their 4 expression negatively are opinionated, stubborn, humorless, and discouraging.

People with a 5 expression number are adaptable, adventurous, and versatile. They are not always good at taking advice and prefer instead to learn from experience. Their reluctance can create problems at times, but they're positive people who bounce back quickly after any setbacks. They are good at selling and any other occupations that involve dealing with others. They can achieve almost anything they set their minds on. People who use their 5 expression negatively are impatient, irresponsible, and thoughtless, and can be overly self-indulgent.

People with a 6 expression number are sympathetic, helpful, nurturing people who work well in fields involving helping others, such as teaching, nursing, and working for the betterment of humanity. They possess integrity and often find themselves in positions of importance in the community. They are generous, understanding, and responsible. People who use their 6 expression negatively can be overly self-sacrificing and suffer from anxiety and worry.

People with a 7 expression number have a dignified, logical approach to everything they do. They often become researchers or educators, as they enjoy studying and learning. They have a slightly different approach to everything they do that can make it hard for people to get close to them. They're often interested in philosophical, spiritual, and psychic pursuits. People who use their 7 expression negatively find it hard to trust others and seem aloof, unemotional, and solitary.

People with an 8 expression number are ambitious, reliable, and efficient, with a realistic approach to life. They're good at dealing with money and have the potential to do well financially. They possess plenty of energy and drive. People who use their 8 expression negatively are stubborn, intolerant, materialistic, and impatient when their progress is slower than they think it should be.

People with a 9 expression number are natural humanitarians with a sympathetic, compassionate, empathetic, philanthropic, and loving approach. They enjoy working in fields that give them the opportunity to help, teach, and inspire others. People who use their 9 expression negatively are selfish, insensitive, and distant.

People with an expression number of 11 are capable at whatever career they pursue but are happiest in fields that enable them to inspire and help others. They are spiritual, intuitive, and idealistic. They love beauty in all its forms. People who use their 11 expression negatively are overly sensitive, self-centered, impractical, and temperamental. They dream of what life should be like but seldom act on these beliefs. Their nervous tension is usually obvious to others.

People with an expression number of 22 are practical, capable, and enterprising. They have a unique approach to problem-solving that provides them with unusual and creative solutions to problems. Their willpower and tenacity ensure they never give up, and they frequently inspire others. They have the potential to work for all humanity. People who use their 22 expression negatively can be eccentric, selfish, and dominating. Problems with nervous tension can make it hard for them to achieve their goals.

Chapter Four
THE SOUL URGE NUMBER

The soul urge number reveals the person's innermost motivations and nature. It's what the person really wants to do, be, or have. It influences, consciously or unconsciously, everything the person does. This number is often hidden from everyone except close family and friends. Some people are unaware of the qualities of their own soul urge until it is pointed out to them. This is because they haven't paused to listen to the call of their souls.

Your soul urge number reveals your innermost motivations. It is derived by turning the vowels in your name into numbers, adding them together, and then reducing them to a single digit or master number. In calculation, the letter Y is considered a vowel if it acts as a vowel in the name and its presence affects the pronunciation of the name. People with an 8 soul urge are ambitious and have a strong desire to make money and be successful in life. They want to use their confidence, energy, and good judgment to achieve their goals. They have plenty of stamina and energy and are able to remain calm even in stressful situations.

The soul's urge is derived from the vowels in the person's full name at birth. They include the usual A, E, I, O and U, but also include the letter Y when it acts as a vowel. If the Y is pronounced, as it is in the name Yolanda, it's considered to be a consonant. If the Y acts as a vowel, as it does in Yvonne, Cynthia, Bryony, Kyle, and Barry, it's considered a vowel. Furthermore, Y is considered a consonant if it is next to a vowel and its presence doesn't affect the pronunciation of the word, for example in the name Kay.

••• EXERCISE THREE •••
How to Determine Your Soul Urge Number

Let's use an imaginary person called David Conrad Jones for our example. Start by turning all the vowels in David's name at birth into numbers, and then reduce them down to a single digit or one of the two master numbers, 11 and 22 using the chart on page 52. Work out the numbers for each word in the name separately, and add them together when they've all been reduced to a single digit:

DAVID—A, I

$1 + 9 = 10$

$1 + 0 = 1$

CONRAD—O, A

6 + 1 = 7

JONES—O, E

6 + 5 = 11

Add the three together: 1 + 7 + 11 = 19

1 + 9 = 10

1 + 0 = 1

The Master number 11 in David's last name is not reduced to a single digit.

David's soul urge number is 1.

What Your Soul Urge Number Reveals

People with a soul number of 1 want to be independent and free to lead life as they choose. They seek opportunities to progress and want to control large-scale endeavors. They need to be in charge and don't like taking orders or being told what to do by others. They are individualistic, loyal, and honest. They are good at coming up with ideas and can clearly see whatever it is they desire in their minds. However, they usually need help with the details.

People with a 2 soul urge desire companionship, affection, friendship, and love. They enjoy being part of a harmonious team and tend to avoid leadership roles. They're sympathetic, sensitive, diplomatic, and tactful. They use gentle persuasion to achieve their goals. They find it hard to conceal their emotions and are sometime hurt by people lacking their sensitivity and awareness.

People with a 3 soul urge want beauty, happiness, and joy in their lives. They want to be involved in a wide variety of fun activities with their friends. They need to be involved in some form of self-expression, especially activities that use words; usually that means talking, and most are therefore good conversationalists. Their goal is to make everyone feel as happy as they are, and they put a great deal of time and effort into achieving this. They are friendly, outgoing, positive people who bounce back quickly after setbacks.

People with a 4 soul urge want to be involved in steady, orderly activities. They are plodders who want to work at their own pace, and they dislike being pushed or hurried. They enjoy routine and dislike rapid changes or not knowing where they stand. They are conscientious, responsible, and practical. They are well-organized, good with details, and prefer to finish what they start.

People with a 5 soul urge want freedom, variety, change, travel, and excitement. They're enthusiastic, versatile, adaptable, and young at heart. They believe that life needs to be lived to the fullest. People with a 5 soul urge are mentally agile and need constant mental stimulation, which provides them with the variety they crave as well as a constant flow of new ideas to explore.

People with a 6 soul urge want to be respected for their responsible approach to home and family life. They want to give and receive friendship, joy, understanding, and love. They have a strong desire to serve and help others. They want to live and work in pleasant, attractive environments and demonstrate their creative and artistic potential in some way.

People with a 7 soul urge rarely show their feelings. They prefer spending time on their own to think deep thoughts and gain insights, understanding, and wisdom. They crave peace and quiet. They have a strong desire to develop their special skills and talents, which range from scientific and technical subjects to spirituality and the psychic world.

People with an 8 soul urge are ambitious and want to make money and be successful in business or politics. They want to use their confidence, energy, good judgment, and business skills to organize and lead others. They have plenty of stamina and energy and can remain cool-headed even in difficult situations. They often need to learn how to recognize and include the needs of others in their plans.

People with a 9 soul urge are natural humanitarians who want to give of themselves in a philanthropic or creative way. This is not easy to achieve as there is likely to be conflict between their personal ambitions and spiritual aims. They are warm-hearted, loving, and kind. They are also imaginative, intuitive, and creative.

People with an 11 soul urge want to share their idealistic and intuitive ideas with others and give of themselves to humanity. They want to create a better future for everyone. They need to make sure that they don't spend so much time dreaming about what they're going to do that they neglect to work on achieving their goals. They are spiritual and highly intuitive.

People with a 22 soul urge want to use their talents in a field that will help mankind progress in a humanitarian way. They want to make an important contribution to the world and would like to be leaders who would help people on an international scale. To achieve this, they need to remain firmly focused on their goals.

How to Determine Balance in the Chart

Now that you know the three major numbers in your char—your life path, expression, and soul urge—you can determine how balanced your numbers are.

If your life path, expression, and soul urge numbers are reasonably close together, such as a life path of 3, an expression of 2, and a soul urge of 5, your chart is considered well-balanced. This means you'll be able to achieve whatever it is you want out of life without too many problems.

If these three numbers are well apart, that's known as a stretched chart. For example, someone with a life path of 1, an expression of 3, and a soul urge of 9 has a stretched chart. The distance between these numbers creates problems early on in life, and this person would have to work extremely hard to achieve any goals. Someone with a life path of 1 and an expression of 22 would have an extremely stretched chart and would have major difficulties in achieving whatever they desire.

When working out balance, an 11 is considered to be one number above 9, and 22 is one number above 11. This means that someone with a life path of 9, an expression of 11, and a soul urge of 22 would have a balanced chart.

A useful way to determine how well-balanced the numbers are is to consider the life path as the person's opportunities in life, the expression as the person's natural abilities, and the soul urge as the person's motivations.

Here's an example of someone with a balanced chart. Michele has a life path of 6, an expression of 3, and a soul urge of 4. This means she'll get plenty of opportunities (6) and has a reasonable amount of motivation (4). She may have to further her education or work on developing her abilities in some other way due to her expression as a 3. With a reasonable amount of effort, Michele should be able to reach her goals.

Paul has a more difficult path. He has a life path of 8, an expression of 11, and a soul urge of 1, which means he has a stretched chart. We can see what problems he's likely to have as he has plenty of opportunities (8), more than enough ability to take advantage of them (11), but virtually no motivation to achieve them (1). He's likely been told from an early age that he's showing great potential, but it won't develop unless he finds someone or something that provides the necessary motivation.

Here's another example. Donna has a life path of 3, an expression of 6, and a soul urge of 9. As these are all creative numbers, it's possible that Donna will choose a career that uses her artistic talents. As 6 and 9 are both caring numbers and 3 loves working with others, Donna may choose a career in a humanitarian field. Whatever career she chooses, the hardest part will be finding suitable opportunities as her life path is 3. She has more than enough ability (6), and an abundance of motivation (9). Once she finds the right opportunity, there'll be no stopping her; in addition to ability and motivation, she has good communication skills (3 and 6) and originality (9).

In the next chapter we'll look at the qualities and traits provided by your day of birth.

Chapter Five

THE BIRTHDAY NUMBER

Your birthday number is the fourth of the four main numbers in your chart, and it modifies and influences the life path number. Of the eleven possible life path numbers, each has thirty-one possible sub-paths depending on the day of the person's birth. Everyone on a 5 life path, for instance, has to learn the major lessons of the number 5, but two people on this path may have completely different sub-paths.

Someone with a 1 birthday number may have been born on the 1st, 10th, 19th, or 28th, and each provides slightly different sub-paths. Someone born on the 19th of the month, for instance, would be a 1 but with a degree of 9 energy added. Someone born on the 1st of the month would possess pure 1 energy with no additional energy from another number.

Your birthday number is the easiest to work out—it is simply the numerical day you were born reduced to a single digit. The exceptions are people born on the 11th, 22nd, or 29th of any month. These are all master numbers, as 29 gets reduced to 11.

Here are the interpretations for each day of birth:

One

People born on the first day of any month are forceful, ambitious, and independent. They're natural leaders who are full of enthusiasm and energy. However, they can be stubborn and find it hard to express their emotions.

Two

People born on the second day of any month are friendly and easy to get along with. They're supportive and caring but can also be nervous and emotional.

Three

People born on the third of any month are positive and upbeat with a strong desire to express themselves in some way. They enjoy raising the spirits of everyone they interact with.

Four

People born on the fourth of any month are determined, stubborn, and energetic. They're efficient, conscientious, and like to finish what they start.

Five

People born on the fifth of any month are versatile, quick-witted, sociable, and in constant search of variety.

Six

People born on the sixth of any month are loving, kind-hearted, and generous.

Seven

People born on the seventh of any month are intelligent, introspective, and idealistic. They have a strong intuition. They need plenty of space and quiet time to recharge their batteries.

Eight

People born on the eighth day of any month are materialistic, productive, and hard-working. They display a sense of status and success even when they're struggling to make ends meet.

Nine

People born on the ninth of any month are creative, generous, giving, and sometimes self-sacrificing. They enjoy learning and passing on their knowledge to others.

Ten

People born on the tenth of any month are determined, ambitious, and creative. They're stubborn once their minds are made up due to a strong sense of where they're heading. They tend to resent anything that might divert them from this.

Eleven

People born on the eleventh of any month are emotional, idealistic, and friendly. Because 11 is a master number, people born on this day experience a great deal of nervous tension.

Twelve

People born on the twelfth of any month are good communicators who are sociable and easy to get along with. They have good imaginations and creative potential.

Thirteen

People born on the thirteenth of any month are hard-working, disciplined, and thorough.

Fourteen

People born on the fourteenth of any month are adventurous and need excitement in their lives as they get bored easily.

Fifteen

People born on the fifteenth of any month are cooperative, knowledgeable, and express their emotions well.

Sixteen

People born on the sixteenth of any month are reserved and can appear aloof. They have a philosophical approach to life.

Seventeen

People born on the seventeenth of any month are practical, conservative, and good at dealing with financial matters.

Eighteen

People born on the eighteenth of any month are extremely capable and enjoy working on large-scale projects. They are natural humanitarians.

Nineteen

People born on the nineteenth of any month are ambitious and motivated. They have strong passions and beliefs along with considerable leadership potential.

Twenty

People born on the twentieth of any month have a strong need for friends, family, and a stable relationship.

Twenty-One

People born on the twenty-first of any month are vibrant, intelligent, and outgoing.

Twenty-Two

People born on the twenty-second of any month are exceptionally capable at anything that interests them. As

22 is a master number, they sometimes experience nervousness and doubts about their capabilities.

Twenty-Three

People born on the twenty-third of any month are sensitive and understanding, and they need a great deal of variety and stimulation.

Twenty-Four

People born on the twenty-fourth of any month are caring, loving, and restless until they find the security they seek.

Twenty-Five

People born on the twenty-fifth of any month enjoy time on their own and develop a deep philosophical awareness of life.

Twenty-Six

People born on the twenty-sixth of any month are generous, open-minded, and receptive to new ideas, and enjoy building up businesses and other enterprises.

Twenty-Seven

People born on the twenty-seventh of any month are responsible, dynamic, and creative. They have high aspirations and tend to be overly critical of themselves.

Twenty-Eight

People born on the twenty-eighth of any month are affectionate, independent, and money-oriented.

Twenty-Nine

People born on the twenty-ninth of any month are inspirational dreamers. As 29 reduces to 11, this is a master number, which creates nervousness and strong emotions.

Thirty

People born on the thirtieth of any month enjoy expressing themselves creatively. They enjoy being busy but often find themselves trying to do too many things at the same time.

Thirty-One

People born on the thirty-first of any month are adaptable, hard-working, and sometimes unreasonable, as they sometimes speak before thinking matters through.

Chapter Six

HOW THE FOUR MAIN
NUMBERS WORK TOGETHER

Now that we've looked at the four main numbers in a numerology chart, it's time to see how they get along with each other. Some combinations of numbers harmonize well, and others can be potentially discordant.

Here's an example of a combination that is usually harmonious. Most of the time, 6 and 9 get on extremely well. Both are creative numbers, and having both numbers in a chart considerably enhances the person's creative abilities. They are also both responsible and concerned about the well-being of others. The 6 gives to others due to its loving, affectionate, and responsible nature. The 9 is giving because it has a strong humanitarian nature and has a need to give of itself to others. However, people with this 6-9 combination must also remain aware of their own needs as they run the risk of constantly helping others and having no time left for themselves.

Here's an example that's generally discordant: 6 and 7 usually find it hard to work together. The 6 is open, friendly, and loving. It enjoys helping and caring for others. The 7 is inward looking and interested in studying, learning, and analyzing. It often develops spiritually and gradually gains knowledge and wisdom. The 6 needs people, while the 7 craves solitude. These two aspects of the same person find it hard to get on, as they're heading in completely different directions.

People with harmonious combinations between the four main numbers generally have easier lives than people with difficult aspects in their charts. That said, those with harmonious combinations may not achieve as much; because life is generally smoother for them, they don't experience much challenge. People who overcome difficulties often develop perseverance and determination that help them to aim high and achieve their goals. Most people have a mixture of harmonious and difficult aspects in their makeups.

Aspects to Number One

1:1   When the same number appears more than once among the four main numbers, it's always discordant. One is the number of independence and is inclined to be self-centered. When two 1s appear together, the person is likely to be egotistical and have little interest in the needs of others. A few people with two 1s in their chart are timid and fearful. The solution is for the person to learn to relax and feel comfortable in group situations.

1:2   This combination is usually difficult; the 1 wants to control and lead, while the 2 wants to be liked but is easily hurt by others' comments and actions. However, this aspect can work as long as the assertiveness of the 1 is kept in check and allows the 2 to use its natural ability to relate well to others.

1:3   This is usually a harmonious combination. The self-seeking nature of the 1 is softened by the ability of the 3 to get along well with others. The communication skills of the 3 complement the 1's ability to lead and organize.

The four main numbers in your chart (life path, expression, soul urge, and birthday) create what are called aspects to each other. These can be positive or negative—each number harmonizes well with some other numbers, but no number relates well to all of the other numbers. People with numbers 1 and 8 as two of the main numbers in their chart usually find it to be a highly positive aspect because the executive and financial skills of the 8 can help the 1 achieve its goals. Although it is rare, it's possible for the 8 to be stubborn and the 1 to be self-centered. On these occasions, even a good and positive aspect can create problems.

1:4   This combination is usually a good one. The 1's ability to control and manage is enhanced by the 4's ability to work hard and create an effective, practical organization. However, this combination can be negative when the 4 is stubborn and rigid.

1:5   This combination is just as likely to be harmonious as it is difficult. The versatility of the 5 can help the 1 achieve its goals. However, the goal-oriented focus of the 1 can conflict with the desire of the 5 for constant variety and change.

1:6   This is a discordant combination; the self-centered nature of the 1 doesn't relate to the desire of the 6 to be responsible and caring for others. This aspect can be made to work if the self-sufficient 1 is prepared to put time and energy into home and family life.

1:7   This combination is usually difficult; the desire of the 1 for attainment conflicts with the more introspective desires of the 7. Sometimes, though, the 1's attainment potential can be enhanced by the unique point of view provided by the 7.

1:8   This is usually a highly positive combination, as the executive and financial skills of the 8 can help the 1 attain its goals. Occasionally, the stubbornness of the 8, combined with the self-centered nature of the 1, can create problems.

1:9   This is usually a difficult combination, as the self-centered nature of the 1 clashes with the giving nature of the 9. However, if the giving of the 9 is expressed through some form of creativity, the 1's attainment potential can help the 9 achieve success.

1:11   This is a difficult combination. Firstly, the two numbers are highly stretched. Also, the self-centered, attaining, independent potential of the 1 conflicts with the idealistic and spiritual potential of the 11.

1:22   This is the most stretched combination possible. The self-centered and independent approach of the 1 frequently interferes with the potential of the 22 for significant achievement and success. Occasionally, the leadership qualities of the 1 can work with the 22 to achieve significant results.

2:1   *See 1:2.*

2:2   It's always a difficult combination when two of the four main numbers are the same. Two 2s usually create someone who interferes in matters that don't concern them, adding further disruption to the situation. They are often impatient. Some 2:2s are introverted and shy.

2:3   This is usually a good combination. The potential of the 2 for cooperating and getting along with others is enhanced by the 3's positivity and social skills. The relationship skills of the 2 enhance the natural ability of the 3 to relate well to others.

2:4   This is usually a positive combination, as the adaptability and cooperative nature of the 2 is enhanced by the practicality and organizational skills of the 4.

2:5   This is a difficult combination; the skills of the 2 for harmonizing and getting along with others is frustrated with the 5's strong desire for freedom and change. The 5 doesn't like being hemmed in with responsibilities and commitments. This aspect can work so long as the 5 energy always has something exciting to look forward to.

2:6   This is a positive combination as the cooperating skills of the 2 are enhanced by the 6's ability to express affection and desire to help others.

2:7   This is a conflicting combination, as the cooperative, harmonizing potential of the 2 opposes the more introspective potential of the 7. The self-absorbed 7 finds it difficult to cooperate with others. However, this combination can work if the 2 can use its sociable nature to express the knowledge and spirituality that the 7 possesses.

2:8   This is a difficult combination because 8 enjoys being a leader and doesn't usually fit in as a member of a communal group. The 8 wants to achieve financial success and the 2 wants to get along well with others.

2:9 This is a harmonious combination, as the potential of the 2 for harmonizing and getting on well with others is enhanced by the 9's giving nature.

2:11 This is a positive combination due to the potential of the 2 to get along well with others being enhanced by the 11's potential for idealistic and spiritual accomplishment.

2:22 This is a difficult combination, as the potential of the 2 for working well as part of a group impedes the desire of the 22 to achieve something large and worthwhile. 2:22 is also a highly stretched combination.

3:1 *See 1:3.*

3:2 *See 2:3.*

3:3 When both numbers are the same, the combination is difficult. Someone with this combination will be frivolous and lacking in purpose or will find it hard to express his or her emotions.

3:4 This is a difficult combination. The 3 is sociable and creative, while the 4 is rigid and set in his or her ways. However, it's sometimes possible to harmonize the systematic, detailed approach of the 4 with the need of the 3 to express itself creatively.

3:5   This is a positive combination, as the people skills of the 3 are enhanced by the need of the 5 for freedom and variety.

3:6   This is a harmonious combination. The friendly, sociable approach of the 3 enhances the potential of the 6 for close relationships and love. As both numbers are creative, all forms of creativity are enhanced in this combination.

3:7   This is a difficult relationship wherein the extroverted 3 is sociable and friendly, while the 7 is introverted and desires peace and quiet.

3:8   This can be a difficult combination, as the 3 is adaptable and sociable, while the 8 is more rigid and wants to achieve financial success.

3:9   This is a positive combination. The 3 and the 9 both have creative and self-expressive capabilities. The 3 gets along well with others and is able to help the 9 achieve their aim of helping and giving to others.

3:11   This is a good combination as the creative, sociable approach of the 3 helps the potential of the 11 for ethical or spiritual achievement. The lightness of the 3 helps the 11 become less serious and more relaxed.

3:22   This is a difficult combination. In addition to being stretched, the frivolous, fun-loving approach of the

3 opposes the serious desire of the 22 to achieve something worthwhile and important.

4:1   *See 1:4.*

4:2   *See 2:4.*

4:3   *See 3:4.*

4:4   This is a difficult combination due to the doubling up of the 4 energy, which creates a person with a rigid, stubborn approach who is unable to see the viewpoints of others. Sometimes the double 4 creates someone who is disorganized and reckless.

4:5   This is a difficult combination, as the desire of the 4 for system and order constantly conflicts with the equally strong desire of the 5 for constant change and variety. The 4 wants to work hard to ensure a secure future, while the 5 wants to be free of commitments. However, this aspect can work well when the stability of the 4 is balanced by the 5's adaptability.

4:6   This is a positive combination, as the potential of the 4 for hard work and a disciplined approach enhances the potential of the 6 for responsibility and care of others.

4:7   This is a positive combination, as the disciplined approach of the 4 increases the potential of the 7 to gain knowledge and insight.

4:8 This is a difficult combination. The 4's disciplined, hard-working approach should enhance the potential of the 8 to achieve success. Unfortunately, it forms a self-centered individual whose abilities are obvious but who is also obstinate, argumentative, and unreasonable.

4:9 This is a difficult combination, as the fixed, rigid approach of the 4 conflicts with the potential of the 9 for helping and giving to others.

4:11 This is usually a difficult combination in which the rigidity and desire for system and order of the 4 conflicts with the spiritual and idealistic potential of the 11. However, the hard-working potential of the 4 can motivate the rather dreamy 11 to accomplish something worthwhile.

4:22 This is usually a positive combination, as the organizational skills of the 4 can help the 22 accomplish its potential for significant achievement.

5:1 *See 1:5.*

5:2 *See 2:5.*

5:3 *See 3:5.*

5:4 *See 4:5.*

5:5 This is an extremely difficult combination—people with it tend to use their freedom unwisely and often overindulge in physical gratification at the expense of more worthwhile pursuits. Indulgences bring little satisfaction until the person achieves a few goals and starts using their time more wisely.

5:6 This is a difficult combination in which the strong desire of the 5 for freedom and variety conflicts with the potential of the 6 to look after others. This combination works well when the 5 accepts home and family responsibilities and adds adventure and fun to family life.

5:7 This is a difficult combination, as the freedom-loving 5 conflicts with the desire of the 7 for introspective investigation and research.

5:8 This is a difficult combination, as the erratic, freedom-loving approach of the 5 is at odds with the rigid, ambitious 8 and its desire for financial success. 5 doesn't like responsibilities or commitments, while the 8 actively seeks financial opportunities and commitments. This combination works best when the person is self-employed and can make use of the 5's fast-moving, free-wheeling potential along with the 8's financial skills and expertise to achieve success.

5:9 This is a difficult combination, as the need of the 5 for freedom and variety conflicts with the desire of the 9 to help others.

5:11   This is usually a difficult combination, as the freedom-loving 5 is at odds with the potential of the 11 for inward spiritual growth.

5:22   This is a difficult combination as the 5's need for variety, change, and freedom conflicts with the potential of the 22 for major accomplishment and success.

6:1   *See 1:6.*

6:2   *See 2:6.*

6:3   *See 3:6.*

6:4   *See 4:6.*

6:5   *See 5:6.*

6:6   This is an extremely difficult combination. Two 6s means the person with this combination will feel overwhelmed by responsibility and find it hard to look after their own needs because of the never-ending needs of others.

6:7   This is a difficult combination. The 6's potential for responsibility and looking after others conflicts with the introspective need of the 7 to learn and understand. This combination works when the person accepts the responsibilities of family life but is also able to have sufficient time on their own.

6:8   This is a difficult combination wherein the 6 wants to look after others while the 8 wants to achieve financial success. This aspect can work as long as the home and family side of the 6 is considered more important than the 8's desire to make more money.

6:9 This is a positive combination, as the 6 is responsible and wants to look after others and the 9 has a strong humanitarian concern for everyone. This is also a good combination for all forms of creativity.

6:11 This is a positive combination in which the 6's potential for responsibility and concern for others is enhanced by the empathy and desire for spiritual growth of the 11. The nervous tension of the 11 may hamper progress.

6:22 This is a harmonious combination, as the responsibility and concern for others revealed by the 6 is enhanced by the desire of the 22 to achieve something powerful and worthwhile.

7:1 *See 1:7.*

7:2 *See 2:7.*

7:3 *See 3:7.*

7:4 *See 4:7.*

7:5 *See 5:7.*

7:6 *See 6:7.*

7:7 This is a difficult combination. The doubling up of 7 energy means the person will be rigid and reveal little of themselves to others. He or she is likely to appear unusual or eccentric. The doubling up of the 7 enhances the person's desire to analyze, understand, and learn. However, he or she will need to learn to express his or her thoughts and feelings clearly and honestly.

7:8 This is a difficult combination in which the inward-looking 7 conflicts with the 8's strong desire for financial success. This aspect works best when the 7 is able to work with complete autonomy and allows the 8 to achieve financial success in a different or unique way.

7:9 This is a difficult combination, as the quiet, introspective nature revealed by the 7 conflicts with the outgoing, giving nature of the 9. However, as both numbers are empathetic and enjoy helping others, this combination can work well provided the 7 gets sufficient time on its own to study and learn and the 9 can use these findings to help people in need.

7:11 This is a positive combination, as the studious, analytical, and philosophical potential of the 7 increases the potential of the 11 for spiritual growth.

7:22 This is a difficult combination, as the introspective nature of the 7 conflicts with the strong potential of the 22 for significant growth and accomplishment.

8:1   See *1:8*.

8:2   *See* 2:8.

8:3   *See* 3:8.

8:4   *See* 4:8.

8:5   *See* 5:8.

8:6   *See* 6:8.

8:7   *See* 7:8.

8:8   This is a difficult combination that can produce two different results. Usually, the person will be overly materialistic and obsessed with achieving goals. Alternatively, they will have no interest in working hard to achieve their goals (again, materialistic) and will have an impractical approach to life. In both possibilities, the person will be extremely stubborn.

8:9   This is a discordant combination in which the 8 wants to make money but the 9 is more interested in giving to others.

8:11   This is a difficult combination—the 8 is focused on financial success while the 11 wants to develop spiritually and intuitively.

8:22   This is a positive combination, as the 8's desire for financial success is enhanced by the ability of the 22 for significant achievement.

9:1   *See 1:9.*

9:2   *See 2:9.*

9:3   *See 3:9.*

9:4   *See 4:9.*

9:5   *See 5:9.*

9:6   *See 6:9.*

9:7   *See 7:9.*

9:8   *See 8:9.*

9:9   This is a difficult combination both for the person with it and their friends and family. People with a 9:9 combination are either overwhelmed by their desire to give to others or are extremely self-serving and greedy.

9:11   This is a positive relationship wherein the 9's desire for giving is enhanced by the desire of the 11 for altruistic and spiritual progress.

9:22   This is a positive combination as the desire of the 9 to give to others is helped by the 22's capability for substantial success.

11:1   *See 1:11.*

11:2   *See 2:11.*

11:3   *See 3:11.*

11:4   *See 4:11.*

11:5   *See 5:11.*

11:6   *See 6:11.*

11:7   *See* 7:11.

11:8   *See* 8:11.

11:9   *See* 9:11.

11:11   This is a difficult combination that usually creates a person who dreams of achieving great things but almost always in the form of impractical, idealistic castles-in-the-air-type schemes.

11:22   This is a difficult combination. The desire of the 11 for philosophical and spiritual growth is at odds with the desire of the 22 to achieve something big and worthwhile.

22:22   This is a difficult combination, as the potential of two 22s overwhelms people who have this in their chart, making it almost impossible for them to achieve their goals. This combination is particularly hard to work with early on in life, but it can be used to great effect once they have learned how to handle this powerful energy.

To see how the four main numbers interact, we'll start by drawing up Suzanne Kay Roberts' chart. Once again, the numerical values are taken from the chart on page 52: I've drawn the chart with the vowel numbers above her name and the consonant numbers below. As we'll be looking at the consonant numbers later, it's more convenient to draw the chart this way.

$$3 + 1 + 5 = 9$$

$$1$$

$$6 + 5 = 11$$

$$9 + 1 + 11 = 21$$

$$2 + 1 = 3$$

SUZANNE KAY ROBERTS

$$1 + 8 + 5 + 5 = 19$$

$$2 + 7 = 9$$

$$9 + 2 + 9 + 2 + 1 = 23$$

$$19 + 9 + 23 = 51$$

$$5 + 1 = 6$$

To work out her expression number, we add the 3 (vowels) at the top of the chart to the 6 (consonants) at the bottom. This gives us Suzanne's expression number of 9.

Suzanne's soul urge from the vowels is 3.

Let's assume that she was born on April 7, 1995. Her life path number is 8:

$$4 + 7 + 1995 = 2006$$

$$2 + 6 = 8$$

As Suzanne was born on the seventh of the month, her birthday number is 7.

This means that Suzanne's four main numbers are:

Life Path 8

Expression 9

Soul Urge 3

Birthday 7

Let's look at Suzanne's life path number and see how it gets on with her expression and soul urge. Suzanne's life path of 8 shows that she wants to do well financially. However, her 9 expression is more concerned with giving to others. This is likely to cause her problems at times. 9 is an artistic number, and Suzanne could potentially use both numbers by creating something attractive, and then making money from it.

Suzanne is also likely to have difficulty in balancing her 8 life path with her 3 soul urge. Her life path wants to make money, but her soul urge is more concerned with being sociable and having fun. However, if Suzanne used the considerable speaking skills her soul urge provides to make money, she would harmonize these qualities and do extremely well.

Suzanne's life path of 8 is modified by her 7 birthday number. Suzanne's life path is ambitious and wants her to move forward and achieve success, particularly financial success. Her birthday number is introspective and idealistic. It's more interested in developing spiritually than making money. However, as the qualities of her 8 life path are always more influential than the qualities provided by her day of birth, she'll have conflicts between the two numbers but the 8 energies will always overrule the qualities provided by the 7. There are times when her 7 day of birth could help her 8 life path. Suzanne's birthday number shows that she enjoys learning, studying, and researching. What she discovers has the potential to be made into something that makes her money.

We already know a great deal about Suzanne, and a numerologist giving her a reading might give the following in a report:

"The four most important numbers in your chart reveal your purpose in life, your opportunities, your abilities, and your motivation. They're all potentials, and it's up to you what you do with them. Every number can be used positively or negatively, and most of us reflect both positive and negative qualities at different times and in different situations.

"Your most important number is 8, which is your life path. It shows that you have leadership qualities and work hard to achieve your goals. This will become more and more apparent the older you become. You're a good worker and have the potential to do well financially. You may find it hard at times to balance your home life with your career. Like everyone else, you'll face temptations at times, and it's important to work as ethically as possible.

"Your life path number is influenced by your birthday number, which happens to be a 7. This is a much more introspective number than the 8. It often gives an interest in spirituality and the psychic world. It also gives you the capacity to analyze, research, and learn. You could use those qualities to help you progress in your career. 7 and 8 don't always blend well. That can often be a good thing, as people with charts full of numbers that harmonize well don't always achieve much in life as everything comes easily to them.

"Your expression number is 9. This shows that you are an empathetic, compassionate person who enjoys helping others. At times in your life, you'll be involved in the community in some sort of way, possibly helping groups of people, teaching others, or maybe righting a wrong. You'll gain a great deal of satisfaction from doing this.

"You may have already discovered that the giving nature of your expression can clash with the strong desire of your life path to progress in the material world and do well financially. However, the positive disposition of your expression will be able to help you achieve the goals of your life path. It will also ensure that you'll always seek a win-win result in all of your business dealings. The giving nature of your expression may sometimes involve money or some other form of tangible asset.

"Your soul urge number of 3 shows that you have a strong desire to express yourself, and you constantly seek beauty, joy, and fun in your life. Your soul urge doesn't always get on with your life path. It wants you to have a good social life, with plenty of opportunities to talk, laugh, and play with your friends. Your life path, on the other hand, wants to be involved in big undertakings and make money. The adaptability of your soul urge conflicts with the rigid, fixed approach of your life path. If you were involved in a career involving dealing with others, such as sales, the charm and conversational skills of your soul urge would be able to help your life path progress financially.

"You have one extremely harmonious relationship in your chart. This is between your 9 expression and 3 soul urge. Both of these numbers are creative and enhance your ability to appreciate beauty wherever you find it, and to express yourself in a pleasing and charming manner. This enhances your potential to give to others in some way.

"Your soul urge is a low number compared to the numbers of your life path and expression. This shows that motivation can be a problem, especially early on in life. Consequently, you might be well aware of your creative and business skills but display them only occasionally. You'll progress quickly once you harness the considerable potential of your life path, expression, and soul urge."

We now know quite a bit about Suzanne Roberts; she would be an entertaining person to know. She'd express herself well and would have good taste (3 soul urge). She'd be caring, sympathetic, and kind (9 expression). She has good leadership and management skills (8 life path). She might be shy and reserved at times (7 birthday). Suzanne is still young, so most of her thoughts and energies will be devoted to enjoying herself (low soul urge number). However, her executive skills will already be evident.

In the next chapter we'll start looking at the personality number. While not as important as the four main numbers we've already looked at, it adds information that helps build a complete picture of the person.

Chapter Seven

THE PERSONALITY NUMBER

Your personality number reveals how other people see you but is not as important to your makeup as the four main numbers (the life path, expression, soul urge, and day of birth). Though it's the image of yourself that you show to the world, it doesn't necessarily reveal who you really are inside. As it reveals your personality, it shows what other people expect of you. It also enables you to discover how other people see you.

••• EXERCISE FIVE •••

How to Determine Your Personality Number

Your personality number is found by adding up all the consonants in your full name at birth, and reducing them down to a single digit except for 11 and 22. Here's an example:

AMANDA DALE PETERKIN

4 + 5 + 4 = 13

1 + 3 = 4

DALE

4 + 3 = 7

PETERKIN

7 + 2 + 9 + 2 + 5 = 25

2 + 5 = 7

Add all three numbers together:

4 + 7 + 7 = 18

1 + 8 = 9

Amanda has a 9 personality number

What the Personality Number Reveals

People with a 1 personality are likeable, capable, and per-suasive. Others expect them to take a leadership role because they always appear to be calm and in control, no matter what kind of situation they find themselves in. They like to dress well and always portray an image of success.

People with a 2 personality are gentle and easy to get on with. They avoid the limelight and dislike arguments and unpleasantness. They are neat and tidy and may sometimes be accused of fussiness. They dress well and choose styles that don't draw attention to them.

People with a 3 personality are friendly, easy-going, and enjoy being the center of attention. They are good conversationalists and always have something interesting or amusing to say. They are creative and enjoy expressing themselves with their choice of clothes.

People with a 4 personality are conservative, practical, reliable, and conventional. They choose their clothes by the amount of wear they can get out of them rather than by fashion. They are serious, honest, and law-abiding.

People with a 5 personality are curious, restless, and always need something to look forward to. They dress well and like bright colors. They sometimes need to be reminded to dress to fit the occasion.

People with a 6 personality are sympathetic and responsible. They inspire confidence, and they're regularly asked for help or advice. They have a creative flair and enjoy being well-dressed in comfortable clothes.

People with a 7 personality are thoughtful, dignified, and refined. On the first meeting, they can appear aloof but are kind and friendly once they get to know people. They have good taste, reflected in their taste in clothing.

People with an 8 personality are sociable, persuasive, positive, and powerful. They dress well as they want to appear successful and prosperous.

People with a 9 personality are warm, friendly, likeable, kind, and generous. They are compassionate and enjoy helping others. Comfort wins over fashion when it comes to their clothing, though they try to encompass both.

People with an 11 personality are inspirational, spiritual, and believe in equality for all. Others sometimes expect more from them than they want to give, as they're not always as confident as they seem. They like clothes and have an original flair in everything they wear.

People with a 22 personality are capable, honest, diplomatic, and have a strong desire to solve all the problems in the world. They dress conservatively and are willing to pay more for good quality clothes.

Your
personality
number reveals how
other people see you, and is
the image of yourself that you
show to the world. It is derived by
turning all the consonants in your full
name at birth into numbers, adding them
together, and reducing them to a single
digit or master number. Someone with a
personality number of 2 would be kind, gentle,
and easy to get along with. They usually avoid
the limelight and dislike unpleasantness and

arguments. They're neat
and tidy in everything
they do. They dress
well and like good-
quality clothes.

Chapter Eight

THE REALITY AND ACHIEVEMENT NUMBERS

Your reality number, sometimes known as the maturity number, comes into play between the ages of 35 and 50. Its effects can be noticed gradually, but usually it starts in the form of a midlife crisis or a reevaluation of the person's life up until that point. This number is particularly useful in the second half of the person's life as an indication of where the person is heading and their ultimate goal.

Your reality number (sometimes called the maturity number) starts to have an influence on you between the ages of 33 and 50. It shows where you're heading in life and what your ultimate goal is. People with a reality number of 4 will gain more control over their lives at about the age of 33. They'll find good opportunities that will pay off as long as they're prepared to work hard and persist until they reach their goals. They'll also be better organized and find it easier to work within the limits of where they find themselves.

The reality number is formed by adding the life path number and expression number together and reducing them to a single digit (or to an 11 or 22).

Our imaginary Suzanne Roberts has a life path number of 8 and an expression number of 9. Her reality number is 8, as 8 + 9 = 17, and 1 + 7 = 8. In this case, her reality number is already one of her main numbers. This means she'll be able to use her 8 energy more positively in the second half of her life. If her reality number had been different than her four main numbers, she'd gradually become aware of the influence of the new number and learn how to incorporate it into her life. Over time, the quality of this new number would provide great satisfaction and contentment.

What the Reality Numbers Mean

People with a 1 reality number need to learn the lesson of independence. If they haven't achieved it by the age of maturity, they may be forced to stand up for themselves in some way. Once they've achieved that independence, they'll feel free to explore their own interests and may assume a leadership role as a result.

People with a 2 reality number usually start to evaluate their diplomatic and sensitivity skills at the age of maturity. They may overcome acute sensitivity and shyness and gain satisfaction from using their people skills to bring harmony and peace to others.

People with a 3 reality number tend to reassess how they use their self-expression skills at the age of maturity. They will start enjoying life much more and may take up creative interests and associate more with others purely for the fun of it.

People with a 4 reality number will find opportunities at maturity that will pay off with hard work and persistence. They'll find it easier to work within limits and apply system and order to everything they do.

People with a 5 reality number will gain more control over their lives at maturity. Although they'll always be busy, they'll find it easier to use their time wisely and will experience a great deal of satisfaction from their accomplishments.

People with a 6 reality number will evaluate their sense of duty and responsibility at maturity and will make any necessary changes to increase their sense of satisfaction. They'll find it easier to stand up for themselves and will enjoy the pleasures of love, family, and friends while still retaining a keen interest in helping others.

People with a 7 reality number will experience great satisfaction and peace of mind once they reach maturity. They'll be able to share their insights and specialized knowledge with others and will experience considerable spiritual growth.

People with an 8 reality number assess the degree of material satisfaction they've gained from the assets they've earned up until maturity. They'll make changes to ensure that the second part of their life provides opportunities for further financial growth but also allows them to gain respect and recognition from others.

People with a 9 reality number will discover at maturity the special joys that come from helping others and the pure joy of giving. They may become involved with a humanitarian organization, or practice giving on their own. Their service to humankind will be recognized, but their greatest satisfactions will come from within.

People with an 11 reality number will gain an increased awareness of the spiritual side of life when they reach maturity. This will involve a major change of outlook and a great deal of soul-searching. Once they've learned how to balance their material and spiritual sides, they'll experience greater happiness and satisfaction than ever before.

People with a 22 reality number will discover at the age of maturity just how much ability and power they actually possess. They'll have to use this power wisely and behave ethically to achieve their exciting and challenging goals.

The Achievement Number

The achievement number also relates to the second half of life and reveals the person's potential and what they need to accomplish in this lifetime. It's a vitally important number but is seldom given consideration or even notice until the person is in their forties or fifties. At this time, the person will start experiencing tension and a sense of uneasiness until they recognize the need to work on whatever it happens to be.

The achievement number is obtained by adding the day and month of birth together and reducing it to a single digit (or 11 or 22).

Suzanne Roberts was born on April 7 (4 + 7). This means she has an 11 achievement number. The 11 shows that she's capable of making significant progress in her life but is more likely to be an aimless, impractical, idealistic dreamer until she recognizes the special talents, insights, and perceptions that come with her master number.

What the Achievement Number Means

People who have an achievement number of 1 need to make use of their ambition, individuality, originality, and leadership ability in a positive way. Their main challenge is to learn how to handle their egos and improve their low self-esteem. They need to learn compassion, cooperation, and how to work as a member of a team rather than always having to be the leader.

People who have an achievement number of 2 are adaptable, cooperative, kind, and modest. They get along well with others but are often shy and overly sensitive, especially when they're young. They must learn to stand up for themselves, as people will frequently try to take advantage of their good nature.

People with an achievement number of 3 are friendly, loving, and easy to get on with. However, they are sensitive and are concerned about what other people might think about them, which can create feelings of inadequacy and insecurity. Their concern about others' approval becomes less important as they reach maturity, when they start moving forward using their creative and communication skills to progress in life.

People with an achievement number of 4 are willing to work hard to achieve their goals. They often feel frustrated and feel they're not getting the opportunities they deserve. They can also be stubborn and resistant to change. Once they reach middle age, they start becoming more responsible, patient, and practical. They adopt a systematic and helpful approach to problem-solving, and once set on a particular course, they'll pursue it until it becomes real.

In the first half of their lives, people with an achievement number of 5 are restless, impatient, and often want to do too many tasks simultaneously. They find it hard to complete tasks that are unexciting or dull. Coupled with their good people skills, their enthusiastic and positive approach to life enables them to achieve almost anything they decide to do once they reach their forties and fifties. All the way through life they love freedom, change, and variety.

People with an achievement number of 6 start out in life with a strong desire to be responsible for others. They are perfectionists who tend to worry and find it hard to express their own unique personality. Once they reach middle age, they'll find themselves expressing their generous, kind, understanding, and giving natures in a positive way. They gain great pleasure from caring for others and enjoy home and family life.

People with an achievement number of 7 find it hard to express their emotions early in life. It's also common for them to have problems in understanding other people's emotions and be critical. They'll be introspective and enjoy spending time on their own. Once they reach their forties and fifties, they'll start using their sharp minds to research and learn about subjects that interest them. They have the potential to become experts in any subject that interests them and enjoy analyzing and understanding difficult problems. They seldom find it easy to relax in the company of others early on in life but gradually learn how to be poised and sociable as they progress through life.

People with an achievement number of 8 are likely to be overambitious, impatient, and materialistic in the first half of their lives. They want to be liked and often seek praise for everything they do. As they mature, they develop their financial and managerial skills, finding themselves able to use their confidence, reliability, leadership skills, and ambition more effectively than they did in their earlier years. They can use their abilities to progress financially. They usually develop their compassionate and philanthropic sides late in life.

People with an achievement number of 9 work well with others and are sensitive to their needs. They're sympathetic, understanding, kind, and friendly. They fall in love easily and are frequently hurt. Fortunately, they never become cynical, and this aspect of their lives becomes much easier the older they become. As they get into their forties and fifties, they start using their positive qualities to motivate, inspire, and help others. They also develop the compassionate side of their nature, becoming more philanthropic and giving.

People with an achievement number of 11 are always aware of their special gifts but find it hard to put them into practice early on in life. They are overly sensitive and tend to be dreamers who are full of impractical ideas. Once they get into their forties and fifties, they develop a deep understanding of others and use this ability to inspire others with their words and actions. They work well with others but don't always feel fully appreciated, as they have a slightly different, often unusual, approach to everything they do. Their intuition and creativity play an important role in their lives.

People with an achievement number of 22 can achieve anything they desire so long as they use their skills and talents wisely. Often, though, everyone is aware of these people's special skills except them because early on in life, these individuals found it hard to deal with the high-powered nervous tension that surrounded them. Once they reach middle age, they realize they can turn their dreams and ideas into reality and make rapid progress. Once they set their minds on a goal, they work hard until they've achieved it. They usually aim high and, with their humanistic approach, achieve many goals that benefit their local communities and even humanity as a whole.

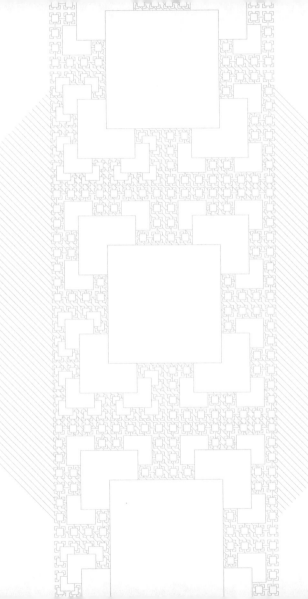

Chapter Nine
THE CHALLENGE NUMBERS

Challenges are the stumbling blocks or obstacles that everyone experiences as they go through life. Learning how to deal with and make constructive use of them helps the person's growth and development. In numerology, there are four challenges worked out from the person's full date of birth.

The challenge number predicts what challenges the person will face at different stages of life.

1 and 2 are the most common challenge numbers, followed by 0 and 3. 4 and 5 are found less frequently, and 6, 7, and 8 challenges are found rarely.

• • • Exercise Six • • •

How to Work Out Your Challenge Numbers

The first step is to reduce the person's month, day, and year of birth to single digits. This produces three single-digit numbers, one each for the month, day, and year of birth. This is one of the few times when master numbers are reduced to a single digit. Here's an example:

February 21, 1995

Month: 2

Day: $2 + 1 = 3$

Year: $1 + 9 + 9 + 5 = 24$

$2 + 4 = 6$

The next step involves subtraction. Interestingly, this is the only time in numerology where numbers are subtracted. For the first challenge, subtract the month digit from the day digit (or the day from the month if the month number is higher). In the above example:

3 (day) − 2 (month) = 1 (First challenge number)

The second challenge number is created by subtracting the day number from the year number (or the other way around, if necessary):

6 (year) – 3 (day) = 3 (Second challenge)

The third challenge, usually called the major challenge, is found by subtracting the first challenge number from the second, or the other way around, if necessary:

3 (second challenge) – 1 (first challenge) = 2 (Major challenge)

The fourth challenge is found by subtracting the month number from the year number (or vice versa):

6 (year) – 2 (month) = 4 (Fourth challenge)

Unusually for numerology, there are no fixed timing dates for the challenges. Some people learn how to deal with their challenges quickly, while others take decades to resolve them. The first challenge starts at the time of birth and is usually learned by the time the person has reached his or her mid-thirties. The second challenge continues from the mid-thirties to the early to mid-sixties. The third challenge is the major life challenge, which lasts throughout the person's life. The fourth challenge starts sometime in the sixties and continues for the rest of the person's life.

In the example above for someone born on February 21, 1995:

Challenge number 1: birth to about mid-thirties

Challenge number 2 is 3: mid-thirties to mid-sixties

Challenge number 3 is 2: main challenge in life

Challenge number 4 is 4: sixties until the end of life

Many people have zero as a challenge number, but it's impossible to have a 9 because 9 is the highest single-digit number and it is therefore impossible to subtract any single-digit number from it and have a total of 9.

It's common for challenge numbers to be repeated; here's an example. The person in the following example has a 3 first challenge, an 8 second challenge, a 5 major challenge, and another 5 for her fourth challenge.

April 28, 1980

Month: 4

Day: 2 + 8 = 10

1 + 0 = 1

Year: 1 + 9 + 8 + 0 = 18

1 + 8 = 9

3 8 (First and second challenges)

5 (Major challenge)

5 (Fourth challenge)

It's also possible for some people to have a zero number in every position. Here's an example:

May 5, 2003

Month: 5

Day: 5

Year: 2 + 0 + 0 + 3 = 5

0 0 (First and second challenges)

0 (Major challenge)

0 (Fourth challenge)

Table of Challenges

0: THE CHALLENGE OF CHOICE. This is the only time in numerology where a zero is used. People with this challenge frequently have difficulty in making decisions. Although they can reason things out, they're apt to be indecisive when it's time to finally decide. They need to have faith in themselves and learn to analyze, choose, and then act. The more they follow through, the easier it will become. Some numerologists claim that a zero challenge is an indication of an old soul, someone who has experienced—and passed—all the other challenges.

This may be the case if zero is the major challenge but is unlikely if it's one of the minor challenges.

1: THE CHALLENGE OF INDEPENDENCE. People with this challenge will find people trying to force them into their way of thinking and acting, leaving little room for their own individuality to grow. They may feel dominated or insecure and try to please everyone, with unsatisfactory results. They could feel that their best is never good enough. They need to learn to let go of resentments and grudges, stand up for themselves and their convictions, and move forward in the direction they want to go. Once they overcome their confidence issues, they'll be able to set bolder goals than ever before.

2: THE CHALLENGE OF OVERSENSITIVITY. People with this challenge will be overly sensitive and easily hurt. This makes it hard for them to cooperate and work with others, as they're reluctant to get involved due to a fear of getting hurt. As they learn to use their sensitivity positively, they'll gain added strengths and awareness, making it easier to cooperate and relate well with others.

3: THE CHALLENGE OF SOCIABILITY. People with this challenge are shy, nervous, and reserved in social situations. They're likely to hide their creative abilities as well. They need to practice the art of communication, develop their conversational skills, meet more people, and try to be more outgoing and sociable. Once they're on this positive path, their optimism and enthusiasm can be a source of pleasure and strength to others as well as themselves.

4: THE CHALLENGE OF SELF-DISCIPLINE. People with this challenge will be reluctant to apply themselves at work. They'll be either good with details or overlook them completely. They're likely to be rigid, stubborn, and uninterested in others' points of view. To overcome this, they need to apply themselves and develop patience, tolerance, and the ability to work as hard as necessary for what they want.

5: THE CHALLENGE OF FREEDOM. People with this challenge will be impatient and inconsistent and feel tied down by routine tasks and responsibilities. They'll find it hard to take advantage of opportunities and will skim rapidly from one interest to the next. They must learn to choose their opportunities with care, finish what they start, and curb some of their natural restlessness.

6: THE CHALLENGE OF INTOLERANCE. People with this challenge need to learn to accept things as they are. They're likely to have high standards and may appear intolerant and controlling to others. They need to learn that perfection doesn't exist and that others have a right to their points of view. They must pay particular attention to harmony in their home and family life and express their innate love for all humanity.

7: THE CHALLENGE OF UNDERSTANDING. People with this challenge may be critical, lonely, and fearful. They probably feel uncomfortable in social situations due to their reserved nature, and they find it hard to express their innermost feelings. They need to develop faith in themselves and their abilities to grow in knowledge and wisdom as well as to feel happy and relaxed in the company of others.

8: THE CHALLENGE OF MATERIALISM. People with this challenge will be totally focused on attaining money, power, and security. As they mature, they gradually learn that achieving more and more wealth doesn't bring long-term satisfaction. They need to learn a sense of proportion, avoid greed, and be scrupulously honest in all their dealings.

9: THERE IS NO 9 CHALLENGE.

Challenges are the obstacles that everyone experiences as they go through life. Learning how to deal with these helps people's growth and development. The four possible challenge numbers a person can have are worked out by a process of subtracting the numbers in their full date of birth. People with a 1 challenge need to learn how to stand up for themselves and move forward in the direction they want to go.

Chapter Ten

THE PLANES OF EXPRESSION

The planes of expression provide further insight into people's character and help explain why everyone has their own distinctive personality and abilities.

Everyone is made up of a mind (mental), a body (physical), a heart (emotional), and a spirit (intuitive). These four qualities create the four planes of expression, which are created from the numbers in the person's full name at birth.

The Mental Plane

The mental plane relates to the person's mind and reasoning ability. It collects all the details and other information necessary to make a decision and then acts on it in a cool, calm, straightforward way. It is logical, analytical, determined, and positive.

The Physical Plane

The physical plane rules over what can be touched and experienced directly. It keeps the person's feet on the ground and governs common sense, practicality, and the instinct to make decisions.

The Emotional Plane

The emotional plane relates to the use of emotions, feelings, inspiration, and imagination to create an environment that is beautiful, compassionate, and happy. On this plane, logic and facts are less important than creativity, laughter, and beauty.

The Intuitive Plane

The intuitive plane represents the spiritual side of the person's makeup. It uses intuition and inner knowing to gain access to the Divine. It is full of compassion and enables the person to express their spiritual insights in the other planes.

How to Determine Your Planes of Expression

All the 1s and 8s in the person's full name at birth (A, H, J, Q, S, Z) belong to the mental level. This is because 1 is the number of independence and attainment and 8 is the number of confidence and material gain. Both numbers use the power of thought extensively.

All the 4s and 5s in the person's full name at birth (D, E, M, N, V, W) belong to the physical level. This is because 4 is a practical, hard-working number, and 5 needs security and the practical world to fund his or her adventures.

All the 2s, 3s, and 6s in the person's name (B, C, F, K, L, O, T, U, X) belong to the emotional level. This is because all three of these numbers are sensitive, caring, and supportive of others. They are all feeling (emotional) numbers.

All the 7s and 9s in the person's name (G, I, P, R, Y) belong to the intuitive level. This is because 7 is spiritual and wants to discover hidden truths, and 9 is impressionable, selfless, and sensitive.

These letters and the planes of expression they belong to can be seen more easily in this chart:

Mental AHJQSZ

Physical DEMNVW

Emotional BCFKLOTUX

Intuitive GIPRY

Here are Suzanne Roberts' planes of expression. The numbers (e.g., Mental 5) come from counting the letters in each category.

SUZANNE KAY ROBERTS

1381555 217 9625921

Mental 5

Physical 4

Emotional 5

Intuitive 3

Suzanne's planes of expression are average, as the different planes vary by only one or two. This is a good thing, as it shows that she is well-balanced and can make good use of all her planes of expression when necessary.

Here's another example.

DEREK JOHN MENDEZ

45952 9685 455458

Mental 3

The
four planes
of expression are
derived from the numbers
derived from all the letters in
the person's full date of birth. They
provide insight into people's characters.
The mental plane relates to the person's
mind and reasoning ability. The physical plane
relates to dealing with what can be touched and
felt. The emotional plane is related to emotions,
feelings, and imagination, and the intuitive plane
relates to the spiritual side of a person's makeup.
People with a predominant physical plane compared

to other planes are happiest
when working with their
hands, while people with
predominant mental
planes gain satisfac-
tion from using
their brains.

Physical 9

Emotional 2

Intuitive 1

Derek's physical plane heavily outweighs the other three planes of expression. This shows that he lives in a world of facts and information that can be proven and demonstrated. He has little time for imagination and keeps his feet firmly on the ground. He prides himself on his common sense and practical approach to life.

Here's an example of someone who has a 0 as one of her planes of expression.

JANE MABEL FOX

1155 41253 666

Mental 3

Physical 4

Emotional 5

Intuitive 0

The zero doesn't mean that Jane lacks intuition; she'll trust her intuition at times. However, in most situations she'll automatically use her other planes of expression.

There's nothing wrong in lacking a number or having a low number in any of the planes of expression. In fact, knowing this can be useful. If you were planning to employ someone as an accountant, you'd do well to employ someone with a high mental number compared to the other planes. If you wanted someone to sell high-quality clothing, someone with a high emotional number might be a good choice. For example, if you wanted someone to renovate a house, Derek would be a good choice due to his high physical plane amount.

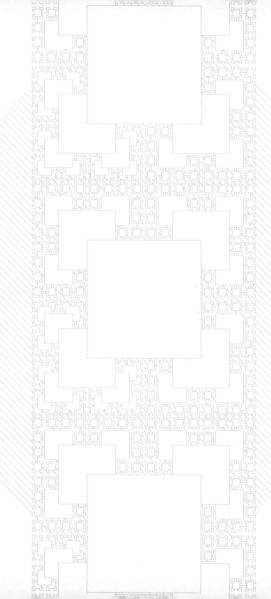

Chapter Eleven
THE INCLUSION

I f you believe in reincarnation, your past life experiences are revealed by all the numbers that make up your full name at birth. This process is called the inclusion. Even if you don't believe that you've lived before, you'll find this exercise a useful way to explore your personality in greater depth. The inclusion reveals experiences that you've encountered many times before (your intensification number) and how you react during times of crisis (called your subconscious response).

Start by making a list of all the numbers in your full name. (These are the same numbers that comprise your expression.) Here are Suzanne Roberts' numbers:

SUZANNE KAY ROBERTS

1381555 217 9625921

One: 4 (SAAS)

Two: 3 (KBT)

Three: 1 (U)

Four: 0

Five: 4 (NNEE)

Six: 1 (O)

Seven: 1 (Y)

Eight: 1 (Z)

Nine: 2 (RR)

In an average name of eighteen letters, the usual quantity for each number is:

One: 3

Two: 1

Three: 1 or 2

Four: 1

Five: 3, 4, or 5

Six: 1 or 2

Seven: 0 or 1

Eight: 1

Nine: 3

Lessons to Be Learned

Glimpses of your past lives are revealed through any missing numbers in your name, indicating lessons that need to be learned, often in difficult or even painful ways. These lessons are considerably modified if the missing number is present as one of the four main numbers (life path, expression, soul urge, or day of birth). If the missing number is not the same as one of the four main numbers, it means it is a lesson that the person has not experienced in a previous lifetime.

Suzanne Roberts has a past life lesson of four, as she has no 4s in her full name at birth. As 4 is not one of Suzanne's four main numbers, the karmic lesson isn't modified. (Her life path is 8, expression 9, soul urge 3, and birthday 7.) This means she'll be experiencing this past life lesson for the first time in this lifetime.

Past Life Lesson Numbers

One is the number of independence and attainment. People who lack a 1 will have failed to use their initiative or independence in a previous life. In this lifetime they'll lack confidence, feel unsure of themselves, and lack energy and drive. They'll also find it hard to stand up for themselves. They need to learn to trust themselves, make decisions, and then act on them.

Two is the number of tact and diplomacy. People who lack a 2 will have lacked tolerance in a previous life and may still show a lack of consideration for others in this lifetime. They'll be so sensitive that they'll find it difficult to cooperate or make friends with others. They'll need to learn how to get on with others and value other people's feelings and opinions.

Three is the number of creative self-expression. People who lack a 3 will have been shy and timid in a previous lifetime. They'll be withdrawn, avoid social activities, and under-rate their creative abilities. They'll need to learn to express their feelings openly and show the world how much joy and creativity they possess.

Four is the number of work. In a past life, people who are missing a four will have been disorganized and impatient. When it's missing in this lifetime, the person will dislike work and will try to avoid it whenever possible. There's usually a strong dislike of manual or detailed work. However, it's rare for someone to totally lack the number four anywhere in their chart, as it's essential for accomplishing anything worthwhile. Someone who is missing a four will need to learn the advantages of organization and self-discipline to achieve their goals.

Five is the number of freedom and variety. People who are missing a five feared taking risks in past lives and were unable to use their time wisely or productively. People who are missing this number find it hard to accept change, dislike large gatherings of people, and avoid new opportunities. It's rare for this number to be totally lacking in a chart, as everyone possesses curiosity and needs variety in life. The lesson is to learn from all the changes that occur and to make the most of this lifetime.

Six is the number of home and family responsibilities. People who are missing a six will have been irresponsible, reckless, and selfish in a past life. People lacking this number will have problems with duty and responsibility. They'll be constantly disappointed at the lack of perfection in others, especially in close relationships. The lesson is about accepting responsibility and caring for those who need help.

Seven is the number of spirituality and wisdom. In a past life, people who are missing a seven were knowledgeable and wise but chose not to share their wisdom with others. They'll have no interest in religion or the occult and are likely to be intolerant and impetuous. However, they're often happier than people with a number of sevens in their name because they're open-minded and don't need to analyze or overthink situations. It's common for this number to be missing, and many people without it will try to build a sense of faith on their own. The lesson is to pay attention to hunches and feelings as well as to share thoughts and insights with others.

Eight is the number of money and material freedom. In a past life, people missing this number were financially comfortable but squandered their money on frivolous activities. When it's missing, they'll either show a total lack of interest in finances or have an excessive desire to become wealthy. In both situations, they'll feel dependent on others to achieve their goals. The lesson is to look after their own resources in this lifetime.

Nine is the number of the humanitarian. In a past life, people who are missing a nine withheld love, avoided emotional involvements, and felt isolated and alone. When it's missing, it's a sign that these people have yet to learn the lessons of caring, compassion, and forgiveness. They won't feel the need to give to others that is one of the main characteristics of number nine. It's rare for this number to be missing. The lesson for people who are missing this number is to be patient, understanding, and caring, and to express their feelings openly and honestly.

Intensification Number

When someone has a large amount of a particular number or numbers in their inclusion, it increases the qualities of that number, which is why it's called the intensification number.

Most people don't have an intensification number or numbers. When they appear, it's a sign that they've already learned the lessons of that number or numbers in previous lifetimes. Consequently, they find the particular ability or talent easy to access and work with, because they've learned it many times before. There's a risk, though, as they may feel overly confident and make mistakes. Here's an example.

SIMON ALAN SHAKESPEARE

19465 1315 18125175195

One: 7

Two: 1

Three: 1

Four: 1

Five: 5

Six: 1

Seven: 1

Eight: 1

Nine: 2

Simon has an intensification number of 1, as there are so many 1s at the expense of the other numbers. He has already learned the lessons of standing on his own two feet and achieving independence. He'll have many original ideas and his leadership capabilities will be apparent to everyone in this lifetime. However, he needs to be careful that he's not also inflexible, arrogant, and aggressive, especially when it comes to achieving his goals.

Subconscious Response Number

The subconscious response reveals how people unconsciously react in emergency situations. As with the intensification number, not everyone has a subconscious response number. This number is worked out by subtracting the amount of past life lesson numbers the person has from 9. Suzanne Roberts has an 8 subconscious response number, as she has only one past life lesson number (lacking a 4) in her name.

Here's an example of someone with two karmic numbers (lacking an 8 and a 9):

JAYNE AMY MONTAGUE

11755 147 46521735

One: 4

Two: 1

Three: 1

Four: 2

Five: 4

Six: 1

Seven: 3

Eight: 0

Nine: 0

This means that Jayne has a subconscious response number of 7 (9-2 past life lesson numbers = 7).

Subconscious Response Number Meanings

Each person has only one subconscious response number.

People with a subconscious response number of 3 find it difficult to act, and to speak out, in an emergency.

People with a subconscious response number of 4 become overly cautious and find it hard to act in an emergency. They're likely to become overly concerned with unnecessary and irrelevant details rather than take steps to resolve the problem.

People with a subconscious response number of 5 come up with numerous solutions when they find themselves in an emergency. Unfortunately, they become overwhelmed by the various choices and usually fail to see the best solution.

People with a subconscious response number of 6 take their strong sense of responsibility to an extreme level when they find themselves in an emergency. They become totally concerned with others and pay little attention to their own needs.

People with a subconscious response number of 7 adopt a strongly analytical approach to problems when they find themselves in an emergency. Some try to hide from the problems by overindulging in drugs and alcohol.

People with a subconscious response number of 8 instinctively step into a leadership position when they find themselves in an emergency. They know how to take charge, delegate, and raise the spirits of everyone involved.

People with a subconscious response number of 9 handle emergency situations well, as they have dealt with numerous problems in previous incarnations. This time around, they take responsibility for the well-being of others and act calmly and fearlessly while working on resolving the situation.

Past Life Debts

In addition to the past life lessons created from missing letters in the person's full name at birth, there are also past life debts that are said to have been carried over from previous lifetimes. These are revealed if the numbers 13, 14, 16, and 19 appear in the person's life path, expression, soul urge, or day of birth. These numbers relate to lessons that were not learned in a previous lifetime and need to be worked on in this lifetime. If you don't believe in the concept of reincarnation, these numbers relate to special lessons that a person will have to deal with during their life.

These numbers are especially important when they appear in the person's life path, expression, or soul urge. If, for instance, someone has a life path of 5 and the numbers that create this include a 14, the final result is often written on the chart as 14/5 to indicate the karmic debt.

If the past life debt number is found in the person's life path it will affect every area of his or her life. If it's in the expression, it will affect the person's work and everyday activities. If it's in the soul urge, it will affect the person's hopes, dreams, and emotional life.

If the numbers 13, 14, 16, or 19 appear anywhere else in the chart, they are past life lessons. They appear most commonly in people's day of birth. Past life lessons are testing numbers and show that the person has to work especially hard in the area indicated by the number. Our friend Suzanne Roberts has a past life lesson of 19 in the first name of her personality number. Her past life lesson relates to independence, as 19 reduces to a 1, the number of independence and attainment.

$$3 + 1 + 5 = 9$$

$$1$$

$$6 + 5 = 11$$

Add the three together: $9 + 1 + 11 = 21$

$$2 + 1 = 3$$

SUZANNE KAY ROBERTS

$$1 + 8 + 5 + 5 = 19$$

$$2 + 7 = 9$$

$$9 + 2 + 9 + 2 + 1 = 23$$

Add the three together: $19 + 9 + 23 = 51$

$$5 + 1 = 6$$

Past Life Debt Number Meanings

People with number 13 were lazy and failed to extend themselves and work hard in a previous lifetime. It arises from the self-centeredness of a negative 1 and the superficiality of a negative 3 (the two numbers that make up 13). Consequently, they need to work on self-discipline, set goals, and apply themselves in this lifetime. They must avoid laziness and procrastination. People with a 13 past life debt number often face challenges related to their ambitions and need to learn the power of perseverance.

People with a past life debt number of 14 misused their personal freedom in a past life and lacked self-control. They overindulged at the expense of personal development. It comes from the self-centeredness of a negative 1 and the irresponsibility of a negative 4. People with this number need to learn moderation and avoid self-destructive behaviors. This lesson is usually learned the hard way, through a number of losses, until the lesson is learned.

People with number 16 were proud, arrogant, and power-hungry in a previous lifetime. Others were badly hurt by this behavior, and people with this past life debt number need to avoid manipulating or dominating others and learn humility. It comes from the self-centeredness of a negative 1 and the misuse of love and responsibility of a negative 6.

People with a 19 past life debt number misused power in a previous lifetime. They were self-centered and egotistical. It is made up of the negative 1 (self-centeredness) and the negative 9 (misuse of ambition and opportunities). In this lifetime, people with this number need to learn to be more selfless, compassionate, and considerate of others.

Not everyone has past life numbers in their numerology charts, and even if they do, these numbers are not necessarily as negative as the traditional meanings imply. They simply reveal areas of life where people with them have important lessons to learn. There's no way of knowing when the debts will be collected, but it's usually in the middle period of the person's life. If people with past life numbers work on these challenges, they can progress spiritually, learn the lessons, and lead more fulfilling lives.

Chapter Twelve

THE TRENDS OF LIFE

Throughout history, people have tried to part the veil, so to speak, and see into the future. At some time in their lives, most people have wondered what the future holds for them. Questions such as "Will my marriage last?" and "Is this a good time to find a new job?" are common. Numerology can't provide the specific details of your future, but it can reveal the trends of your life.

Cycles of Experience

We all live our lives in nine-year cycles. One way to look at these is by constructing a chart called the pinnacles or pyramids. This chart is sometimes also called the attainment.

How to Determine Your Pinnacle Numbers

The appearance of this chart gives a strong clue as to how it gained its name.

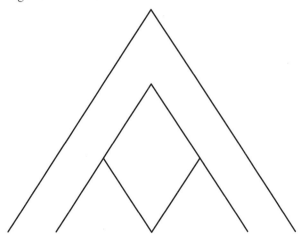

We'll use Suzanne Roberts' date of birth (April 7, 1995) again as an example.

1. Insert the person's date of birth, reduced to single digits or master numbers, beneath the three uprights supporting the inside pyramid. In Suzanne's case, we place the month (April, which is a 4) on the left-hand side, the day (7) in the center, and the year (1995, which reduces to a 6, as $1 + 9 + 9 + 5 = 24$, and $2 + 4 = 6$) on the right.

2. The rest of the chart is completed by doing some simple addition. Suzanne was born on April 7, and consequently has a 4 month and a 7 day. Adding these together gives us 11 (a master number, which means it isn't reduced to a 2), and this is placed at the top of the small pyramid that has 4 and 7 at its base.

3. The next step is to add the 7 (day) and 6 (year) that are at the base of the adjoining pyramid. This comes to 13, which reduces to 4. The number 4 is placed at the top of this small pyramid.

4. We now have an 11 and a 4 at the top of the two small pyramids. We add these together and reduce them down to a single digit (15,

and $1 + 5 = 6$). This number is placed at the top of the center pyramid.

5. Finally, to complete this stage, we add the number of Suzanne's month of birth (4) to the number of the year (6). This totals 10, which reduces to 1. This number is placed at the top of the outer pyramid.

6. The next step is to work out how old Suzanne will be when she reaches maturity, numerologically speaking. This is done by subtracting her life path number from 36. (This means that, in numerology, everyone reaches maturity between the ages of 27 and 35.) Suzanne's life path number is 8. As $36 - 8 = 28$, she reaches maturity at the age of 28. If her life path number had been 11 or 22, it would be reduced to a 2 or 4. This is one of the few times a master number is reduced to a single digit. Suzanne's age at

maturity is placed next to the 11 at the top of the first small pyramid.

7. We continue in nine-year cycles. 28 + 9 = 37, and this age is placed beside the 4 at the top of the small pyramid on the right. 46 (37 + 9) is placed at the top of the inner pyramids, and 55 is placed next to the 1 at the top of the outer pyramid.

8. Finally, you can put the ages 64, 73, and 82 at the base of the two pyramids we began with. In Suzanne's case, 64 would be placed next to her month of birth (4), 73 next to her day of birth (7), and 82 next to her year of birth (6).

These ages mark out periods of time and do not indicate the length of the person's life.

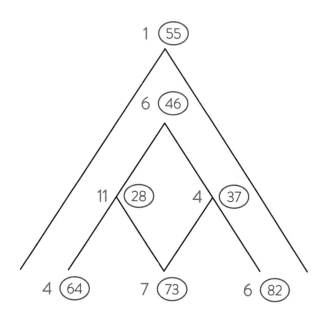

1 (55)

6 (46)

11 (28)   4 (37)

4 (64)   7 (73)   6 (82)

Suzanne's pinnacles can now be read. Numerologically, she reached maturity at the age of 28. This may sound surprising, but in numerology it takes people quite a while to work out what they want to do with their lives and get started on the right path. From birth up to 28, she was heading toward an 11, a master number. Although it is good and strong, unfortunately very few people can handle a master number in the growing up years, and she probably worked at the lower level of a 2. This means she was agreeable and easy to get along with. She's always been sensitive to the feelings and needs of others, and always cooperated and harmonized well with others, which makes her a good friend that gives and receives a great deal of friendship and love. Although she may not have been aware of it, the 11 will have revealed itself from time to time, showing others and herself that she has the potential to achieve great things in this lifetime.

From the age of 28 to 37, she is headed toward a 4, the number of practicality, service, and hard work. This will be a busy period in her life, but by the time she reaches 37 she will have achieved something really worthwhile. It will come solely through hard work and effort. She may feel limited and restricted during this time but the results will make all the effort worthwhile.

From 37 to 46, she is headed toward a 6. Six relates to home and family responsibilities. Ideally, this will be a stable relationship, possibly with children. She will be involved in helping others, especially people who are close to her, which will keep her busy. However, there'll still be time for creative activities, as 6 is one of the three creative numbers.

From 46 to 55, she is headed toward a 1. This is the number of independence and attainment. She will finally have time to stand on her own two feet and achieve something worthwhile. Leadership qualities will become more evident to help her achieve goals.

From 55 to 64, she is headed toward a 4 again. She will be busy and may feel as if she's carrying a large weight on her shoulders. She will not always be able to do what she wants to do because of the needs of others. Despite this, her hard work ethic pays off during this time.

From 64 to 73, she is headed toward a 7. This means she will be doing quite a bit of learning during this time. It could mean continuing her education in some sort of way, or it may be done by reading, meditation, and other forms of study. She is likely to develop spiritually during this period, too. This nine-year period will be a quiet, pleasant, happy time where she will certainly be wiser at the age of 73 than at 64.

From 73 to 82, she is headed toward another 6. As I mentioned earlier, 6 relates to home and family, and she will be closely involved with the special people in her life during this period. It will be a special, loving, and caring stage in life. She will get older surrounded by the people she loves.

This is an example of a quick reading using nothing but the pinnacles. Suzanne's pinnacles are useful, as they include a master number (11 in her case). Master numbers always give the opportunity for great progress, and it's best if they appear in the middle years of the person's life. A master number in the growing-up years is almost always wasted, as hardly any young people can handle the nervous tension and powerful energies of an 11 or 22. Remember that 11 is also the number of daydreaming, so there is no guarantee that the person will make good use of it, no matter where it appears. A 22 is always used.

Suzanne had no consecutive numbers in her chart (the same number repeated in a sequence), which gives the person at least eighteen years of the same energy. This means that the lesson of the number is not fully learned in the first nine years and needs to be repeated.

It's possible for someone to have the same number on every pinnacle. Someone born on September 9, 1980 is an example. Although it would appear at first to indicate a rather sad and tragic life, this is not necessarily the case because you must look at all the numbers in the person's chart. In addition, the quality of the person's life depends on how they use the numbers they've been given.

The Universal Year

We lead our lives in nine-year cycles. The universal year applies to everyone on the planet and is determined by reducing the current year to a single digit. The year 2025, for example, is a 9 universal year, as $2 + 0 + 2 + 5 = 9$. This is a time of completion wherein anything that has outworn its use comes to an end. There'll be an increasing interest in spirituality and religion. People will also start thinking about new large-scale projects that will start in the following year, because 2026 is a 1 universal year in which the nine-year cycle starts again.

There are times in everyone's life when their energies work with them and everything seems to go their way. When the person's life path number is the same as the universal year, they will find that life is easier, as they are unconsciously working with their life path energy in the universal year. Our imaginary friend, Suzanne Roberts, has a life path of 8, which means that life will have been smoother and easier for her in 2024 than it had been for many years.

The Personal Year

In addition to the universal year, everyone has a personal year that also goes in nine-year cycles.

How to Determine Personal Years

The personal year is determined by adding the current year to the day and month of birth and reducing the result to a single digit.

Here's an example using Suzanne Roberts' day and month of birth: April 7, 1995. Let's assume we want to know what her personal year number will be in 2028.

Month: 4

Day: 7

Year: 2028

4 + 7 + 2028 = 2039

2 + 0 + 3 + 9 = 14, and 1 + 4 = 5. Suzanne will be having a 5 personal year in 2028.

The personal years run from January 1 to December 31. However, the influence of the personal year number starts in October of the previous year and gradually gains energy until it is fully apparent by January 1. Similarly, its effect gradually becomes less noticeable from October to December when the influence of the following year's personal number starts to be felt.

The Personal Year Numbers

A 1 personal year marks the start of a nine-year cycle of experience. It's a year of beginnings, so whatever you start now will last for a long time and have a major influence on your life for the next eight years. You'll have plenty of energy and enthusiasm. It's a time to be daring, independent, and courageous. You'll need to show motivation and initiative, as the most important things that happen this year will be the results of your efforts and determination. Set some important long-term goals and start working on achieving them. Expect an important change relating to your career or personal life this year.

A 2 personal year is a time of cooperation and slow, steady growth. It's a year of consolidation in which everything you started in the previous year is brought back to manageable proportions. Whereas in a 1 year you can push and make things happen, that won't happen easily this year. Instead, it's a good year to nurture what you've already started rather than involving yourself in new activities. Tact, diplomacy, and patience rather than force will be required this year.

This is a good year for close relationships in which love is highly favored. Spend time with loved ones, and trust and act on your intuition. You may feel more sensitive and emotional than usual during the year. This is a good year for resolving longstanding difficulties.

A 3 personal year is a light-hearted, carefree, happy year with plenty of opportunities to express yourself creatively and to express all the joys of living. You'll enjoy a good social life and will spend many happy hours entertaining others and being entertained by them in return. It's a good year to make new friends, catch up with old friends, and experiment with new interests. This is also a good year for creative activities, especially those involving communication, such as singing and writing. There are likely to be pressures on your time, but the emphasis this year is on having fun rather than plain hard work.

A 4 personal year is a challenging year involving a great deal of duty, responsibility, and hard work. It's more serious in nature than the previous year, and you'll be spending time creating a good foundation to build your long-term goals on. Pay particular attention to details, and make sure to meet your commitments. This is a particularly good year to set yourself a worthwhile, challenging goal. If you apply yourself, you'll have achieved it by the end of the year. This will bring you great satisfaction. Be cautious with your finances and avoid anything speculative.

Although the emphasis of this year is on hard work and responsibility, make sure to take time out for rest and recreation.

A 5 personal year is a year of change and variety. You need to expect the unexpected and will find yourself enjoying activities you'd never considered before. This is the perfect year to do something you've always wanted to do but never quite got around to doing. It's a good year for travel, especially to places you haven't visited before. Do something different, seize opportunities, enjoy the freedom you have this year, and explore anything that interests you. If you're not doing anything different or exciting this year, you'll feel unsettled and wonder why.

A 6 personal year is a year of home and family responsibilities. This includes your physical surroundings as well as the special people in your life. It's a good year for love and romance—the more you give of yourself, the more you'll receive back in return. It's a good year to start long-term relationships, entertain friends, redecorate your home, and resolve family problems. You may find that people close to you will come to you for help or advice this year, and you'll need to be understanding and compassionate with them. It's possible that you won't be able to do everything you want to this year because of others' needs. Although you'll gain great pleasure from helping people who need your compassion and understanding, don't let yourself be taken advantage of by others, and make sure to stand up for yourself when necessary.

A 7 personal year is a quieter, gentler year, and you will probably seek time to be on your own to meditate, smell the flowers, think about your life and where you're going, and learn and grow spiritually and intellectually. Let other people know when you're planning to spend time by yourself so they'll understand and give you the peace and quiet you need. This is an introspective, non-materialistic year that has its own special rewards. You may have a desire to study and continue your education this year, possibly in technical, scientific, spiritual, or psychic fields. During the year you may experience a number of moments of spiritual insight.

An 8 personal year is the time when you reap the rewards for whatever work you've put in over the last decade. If you've worked hard, you'll experience accomplishment and financial success. Make sure to have a specific financial goal this year, as you'll accomplish it by the end of the year if you're willing to work hard. This is a busy year, full of opportunities, and you'll need to be focused and well-organized to make the most of it.

Make sure to take a vacation during the year, as there'll be a strong temptation to work too hard, and this could affect your health.

A 9 personal year is a transitional year, as it marks the end of the current nine-year cycle and the start of a whole new cycle of experience. Part of you will be looking back and part of you will be looking ahead, making plans for the future. A 9 year is usually a pleasant year, but there'll be odd melancholy moments in which you'll need to let go of activities and interests that have outworn their use. But when you let go, you'll make way for new interests that will come into your life in the next nine-year cycle. Anything new taken up this year is likely to end quickly because this is a year of endings rather than beginnings.

During the year you'll have a number of false leads as to where you want to go from here. However, it will become obvious in the final few months where you want to go and what you want to do next. You may wonder why you hadn't thought of it years ago, but these thoughts occur when the time is right. Some of these endings are likely to be emotional. However, there'll also be celebrations at the accomplishment of goals you've worked on for many years.

It's also a year of kindness and generosity, love and concern, and possibly time for creative activities. You'll also be helping others in charitable activities.

An 11 personal year is a special year in which your intellect and intuition are expanding. You may become interested in spiritual and metaphysical pursuits or pay more attention to the arts than ever before. You'll meet intelligent, perceptive people who'll encourage you to develop your own creativity. However, there's bound to be a degree of nervous tension. During an 11 personal year, you'll also experience the energies of a 2 personal year.

A 22 personal year is a year in which you have the potential for major accomplishment and recognition. Make sure that your goals help humanity and aim high. With hard work, there's no limit to how far you can go.

There's always a degree of nervous tension whenever master numbers appear, and there's a possibility that you'll be emotionally hurt by people who gain pleasure from personal politics. During a 22 personal year, the qualities and attributes of a 4 personal year are also present.

The Personal Month

The number of the personal month provides short-term energy to the personal year.

How to Determine Personal Months

Add the number of the calender month to the number of the personal year, and reduce thc result to a single digit, or master number. Here's an example. Suzanne Roberts was born on April 7, 1995. In 2026, she'll be in a 3 personal year.

Month: 4

Day: 7

Year: 2026

4 + 7 + 2026 = 2037, which reduces to a 3

In January 2026, she'll be in a 4 personal month, as the 3 personal year is added to the number of the month, which is a 1 in January.

This means that she'll be making the most of all the joyful experiences the 3 personal year offers. However, in both January and October, she'll be busy and working hard. Here are Suzanne's personal month numbers for 2026:

Calendar month   Personal year   Personal month

January: 1 + 3 = 4

February: 2 + 3 = 5

March: 3 + 3 = 6

April: 4 + 3 = 7

May: 5 + 3 = 8

June: 6 + 3 = 9

July: 7 + 3 = 10 (reduces to 1)

August: 8 + 3 = 11

September: 9 + 3 = 12 (reduces to 3)

October: 10 + 3 = 13 (reduces to 4)

November: 11 + 3 = 14 (reduces to 5)

December: 12 + 3 = 15 (reduces to 6)

What Personal Month Numbers Mean

A 1 personal month is a good month to start something new, seek out opportunities, and emphasize your individuality and originality. It's a time to be courageous, move forward, take charge, and make a fresh start. This is the perfect month to make any changes that you consider necessary.

In a 2 personal month, you'll need to be quiet, gentle, sensitive, and understanding. Pay attention to details, and check everything carefully this month. You'll also need to be patient and wait for matters in your life to start moving forward again. It's a good month to cooperate with others and be content to work in the background.

An 11 personal month is a more powerful month than a regular 2 month. During this month you may become aware of the spiritual side of your nature, or suddenly sense the interconnectedness of all life. Act on your intuition, as your hunches and feelings will provide you with good ideas this month. You're likely to have some difficult moments, too, as you'll experience increased sensitivity and nervous tension.

A 3 personal month is a good month for social activities and anything else that you enjoy doing. Buy something attractive for yourself. It's a good time for creativity, and you'll be expressing your delight and optimism with everyone you encounter. This is a happy, less serious month. Spend time with friends and make the most of this special month.

A 4 personal month is a time to be serious, practical, and conscientious. You'll need to be well-organized and prepared to work hard to achieve the results you want. You may feel hemmed in and restricted and might find it hard to work within the limits you find yourself within. Make sure to take time for rest and relaxation.

A 22 personal month is a powerful month to work on large-scale concepts and ideas. If you approach the significant opportunities that this month provides in a positive, inspirational way, you'll make great progress. Major tasks that you've been working on for some time may be accomplished this month. The nervous tension that always accompanies master numbers could hold you back during the first two weeks of the month.

A 5 personal month is the perfect time to do something adventurous or different. Anything that takes you out of your normal routine will be good for you. It's an excellent time to make any necessary changes and seek opportunities for excitement and fun. Expect the unexpected and be ready to try anything new, different, or appealing.

A 6 personal month is a rewarding month focused on the domestic side of life. You'll enjoy helping and supporting people close to you and will spread your affection and love everywhere you go. Give advice to people when they ask for it, but don't assume responsibility for anything that belongs to others. It's a good month to use your imagination and do something creative.

A 7 personal month is a good time to pause and make plans for the future. You're likely to spend time reflecting on the spiritual, intuitive side of your life. You'll feel the need for time on your own, and may spend some of it studying, learning, researching, or simply reading. It's a peaceful, quieter, gentler month.

An 8 personal month is a time to move forward and take advantage of any opportunities, especially financial opportunities, that present themselves. You'll feel confident in your abilities and, if you approach everything in a decisive and businesslike way, will be able to make a great deal of progress during this month.

A 9 personal month is a time to help others, and this usually involves giving of yourself in some way. It could be helping people in your local community, righting a wrong, or simply helping people with their problems. It's also a month of endings, making it a good time to finish any short-term projects. It's also a good month for creative activities. As you may feel rather sensitive this month, try to keep emotionally well-balanced and not take any negative comments personally.

How to Interpret Personal Years and Months

Up until now, we've been looking at the personal years and personal months separately. But in practice, we go through all nine numbers at least once every year, and all nine of them influence the personal year number. You would expect a 1 personal year, which is a year of independence, new starts, and opportunity, to begin with a surge of activity. However, January in a 1 personal year is a 2 personal month, which slows down the start of the new cycle. A 1 personal month doesn't occur until September in a 1 personal year.

Here are sample readings for each month of the nine-year epicycle.

One Personal Year

A 1 personal year is a time of new beginnings. It's a good year to get something important underway as you're starting a whole new cycle of experience. You'll need to motivate yourself, as you won't get much help from others. Think, make plans, and only then make your move. There is the possibility of an important change during this year that will be initiated by your own efforts. You'll be working on developing your skills and gaining more independence this year.

January (2 personal month): You'll experience a slow start to the year. Don't worry about it, though. Your energy might be lower than usual, and you could be feeling more sensitive than usual. Keep calm, remain patient, and make plans.

February (3 personal month): This is a good month for mixing with others. You and your friends will enjoy social activities, and it's possible that you'll pick up some ideas and leads at the same time. It's a good month for meeting new people. Some exciting career possibilities might be offered to you this month.

March (4 personal month): Keep your feet on the ground and don't get carried away with ideas that are not practical. Do the work that needs to be done, keep a positive outlook, and expect slow but steady progress. You may feel hemmed in or restricted, but these feelings will be short-lived.

April (5 personal month): You're likely to change some of your plans now and try something new or different. As this is a busy month, you'll need to be attentive and disciplined to make sure that the important tasks get done.

May (6 personal year): Other people will need your help and advice. You may find that you want to stay close to home this month. There'll be obligations that need to be met and a variety of other responsibilities. There could be opportunities for love and romance.

June (7 personal month): Your forward progress slows down temporarily. You're likely to experience delays in business and finance. Remain calm and free of stress. Use the time to look more deeply into your plans. Investigate everything thoroughly.

July (8 personal month): This is a busy month that will bring you closer to your financial and business goals. Seize the opportunities, work hard, and you'll get the results you deserve. If you made plans in June, you'll reap the rewards now.

August (9 personal month): You'll be finishing off projects and enjoying a good social life this month. Give others the benefit of your knowledge and experience. Tie up any loose ends.

September (1 personal month): This is a forward-moving, busy month, and you'll have plenty of enthusiasm and energy to make the most of it. You'll have opportunities to take an important and exciting step forward this month.

October (2 personal month): This month gives you a hint of the direction you'll be taking next year. You'll be working happily and effectively with others. You may have to step back and give other people time to demonstrate their ideas. Keep your emotions in check and don't let any frustration show.

November (3 personal month): This will be a fun month. Avoid scattering your energies over too wide an area. You'll have opportunities to express yourself creatively in enjoyable ways. Enjoy the playful, fun times, but don't neglect your major goals.

December (4 personal month): This will be a busy month of hard work. Be disciplined and well-organized. Make plans for next year and do all the preparations necessary. You may feel you're doing too much when everyone else is slowing down for the holiday season. Get these tasks out of the way, and then enjoy the holiday season.

Two Personal Year

In a 2 year, you have to wait for the results to happen. Don't hurry or try to force things along. Be patient and spend time with the special people in your life. If you're not careful, you may end up sabotaging yourself this year. This is because your energy levels are a little lower, and you may be more sensitive than usual. Keep a low profile and wait for the things that you need to come to you. This is a good year for making new friends and rekindling old friendships.

January (3 personal month): You'll be feeling optimistic and sociable. This is a good month for socializing or possibly taking a vacation. Have fun with friends and get in touch with your sense of humor.

February (4 personal month): Be well-organized, realistic, and practical this month. Work hard, take care of the details, and finish what you start. Make sure to take some time out for rest and relaxation.

March (5 personal month): Expect the unexpected, as you may find yourself doing something new or different this month. Take life as it comes and make the most of any changes that occur. You're likely to travel, meet different people, and try something new. You'll also have opportunities to advance one or more important interests. There is the potential for romance this month and the best results will occur if you let it progress gradually.

April (6 personal month): The emphasis is on your home and family this month. Do what needs to be done in good humor and with enthusiasm. You'll be happy with what you achieve. Enjoy the affection, friendship, and love that comes your way this month.

May (7 personal month): Remain patient despite the delays that are likely this month. Take time to think, analyze, and to make sure that you're moving in the right direction. Think everything through and make plans, but don't act just yet.

June (8 personal month): This is a good month for both making and spending money. Your energy levels are higher again, and you'll feel expansive and upbeat. The hard work you put in this month will pay off over the next few months.

July (9 personal month): You'll be learning and sharing your knowledge this month. This is a good month to complete projects and to make plans for next month. It's also a good time to make new contacts and investigate new opportunities.

August (1 personal month): This is a good time to start anything new. You might pick up a new interest or rediscover an old one. It's a month to move forward positively again. Enjoy the vitality and excitement that will pervade everything you do.

September (2 personal month): Your energies may not be as strong as usual, and you're likely to be feeling sensitive and emotional this month. Remain calm and think carefully before you speak. It's a good month for new and existing relationships.

October (3 personal month): You'll be feeling optimistic and joyful this month. You'll make the most of the pleasant social activities that occur at this time. You'll have fun and be able to express your ideas in a clear and entertaining manner.

November (4 personal month): This is a busy month, and you'll need to be disciplined to handle all the work that needs to be done. Pay attention to the details and be as practical and as efficient as possible. You could make some important decisions this month.

December (5 personal month): This will be an eventful month with a number of changes and plenty of variety. Seize the opportunities that come your way. You may find yourself exploring something new and different.

Three Personal Year

This is a good year to enjoy fun times with friends and to focus on expressing your talents in a variety of ways. You'll feel enthusiastic and full of energy. Friends will bring both fun and business opportunities. You'll feel lighter and freer than you've felt for a long time. You'll be able to express your talents, personality, and ideas effectively. You may receive recognition for your ideas and suggestions. Your friendliness and engaging personality will get you what you want this year. This can be a good year to develop an important creative interest, too.

January (4 personal month): You'll need to be serious, well-organized, and practical to make the most of this month. You're likely to be working harder than you'd like, but don't take shortcuts—the work needs to be done properly. By the end of the month, you'll find that the hard work and effort has paid off.

February (5 personal month): This is a good month to try something new or different. Make the most of any unexpected surprises. You'll have plenty of energy and will enjoy physical activities at this time.

March (6 personal month): This is a caring month and you'll be involved in helping others. You'll probably need to put other people's needs ahead of your own. The focus is on your home, family, and community. Approach everything with a positive state of mind and you'll gain satisfaction and pleasure throughout the month.

April (7 personal month): Your energies will be lower this month, and you'll enjoy quiet, calming times with the people you love. You'll want peace and quiet to think things through and to recharge your batteries. This is a good month for study and learning.

May (8 personal month): This is an action month, and you'll be involved in down-to-earth, practical activities. There'll be financial opportunities to investigate, and you'll need to think quickly and be well-organized to make the most of this dynamic month.

June (9 personal month): This is a good month to tie up loose ends and to make future plans. You'll gain great satisfaction from helping others, or possibly working in the community, during the month.

July (1 personal month): As long as you're motivated, this will be a progressive, dynamic month. It's a good time to use your creativity, intelligence, courage, and intuition to take a big step forward.

August (11 personal month): You'll need to be tactful and patient this month. You may feel tense because your sensitivity is unusually strong. This can be draining, so make sure you get plenty of rest. Your mind will supply you with plenty of ideas this month. Evaluate them carefully, as some will be well worth pursuing.

September (3 personal month): You'll have plenty of opportunities to express yourself this month. The emphasis will be on fun and laughter rather than hard work. Make sure your work commitments are met and try not to overspend this month.

October (4 personal month): This is a practical month, and you'll be working hard. Keep to a regular schedule and make sure you allow time for rest and recreation. Be as efficient as possible and think about what you're doing. You might come up with better ways to do familiar tasks.

November (5 personal month): Try something new this month just for the fun of it. You're likely to find opportunities to combine business and pleasure at this time. This is a good month for a vacation or a few days away.

December (6 personal month): The emphasis is strongly on home and family this month, but there'll be many other tasks that need attending to. Get them out of the way as early in the month as you can. Enjoy special loving times with your friends and family. The holiday season will be particularly pleasant if you ensure that it's spent with the special people in your life.

Four Personal Year

Hard work, conscientiousness, and self-discipline pay off this year. The plans you started three years ago will start producing results and will provide motivation for further progress. Make sure to take time off during the year to rest and relax but keep your eyes firmly on your important goals.

January (5 personal month): Expect your plans to change. You might travel or find yourself doing something totally unexpected. Enjoy social activities and opportunities to meet others. You'll be expressing the joys of life in exciting and unusual activities.

February (6 personal month): This month's focus will be on your home, family, and personal responsibilities. You'll also spend quite a bit of time helping others in some way. Someone may need your help and advice. Be patient with others and avoid misunderstandings.

March (7 personal month): This is a good month to think, study, meditate, and make plans. Develop your self-awareness and think about spiritual matters and your beliefs. Your energy levels are likely to be lower than usual.

April (8 personal month): Your energy levels will be high again, and you'll be focused on money, finances, or business matters. You'll progress quickly this month if you work hard. Ignore timewasters and people who want to pull you down to their level.

May (9 personal month): This is a good month for finishing off projects. You'll be helping people who need advice or a shoulder to lean on. Spend time goal setting and deciding what you want to achieve by the end of the year.

June (1 personal month): You'll have plenty of energy at your disposal this month. It's a good time to start something new, but make sure it's something that excites and energizes you. Assert yourself when necessary and start moving ahead.

July (11 personal month): Keep the peace by holding your tongue when necessary. Concentrate on everything that needs to be accomplished this month. Be patient—it will take longer than you'd like. You're likely to experience a degree of nervous tension. Make an effort to be as positive as you can.

August (3 personal month): This is a good month for socializing, making new contacts, and demonstrating your talents. As the emphasis is on pleasure rather than work, take this time to relax a little and enjoy your hobbies, other interests, and social activities.

September (4 personal month): This is a slow and at times frustrating month. You may feel hemmed in and restricted. Keep busy and look forward to seeing the results of all your hard work by the end of the month.

October (5 personal month): Expect some surprises and unusual experiences this month. Take a break from your normal, everyday activities. There'll be a number of changes, only some of which are planned, this month.

November (6 personal month): You'll want to spend as much time as possible this month at home surrounded by the people you love and care for. This is a good month for doing some redecorating around the house. Nothing will bother you, and you'll have a sense of joy and satisfaction in everything you do.

December (7 personal month): Take some time out this month to think about yourself. Your energy will be down, and you'll want to re-evaluate your progress and work out what you want to do next year. Avoid business and financial matters as much as possible. This is a valuable, quieter month that will help you physically, mentally, and emotionally.

Five Personal Year

After all the hard work you did last year, you'll be ready for the excitement and changes this year promises. A 5 year is when you can potentially do all the things you've thought about but haven't had the time or opportunity to do. A major change is likely, probably in your home, work, or family situation.

January (6 personal month): You'll be focusing on your home and family responsibilities this month. There'll be enjoyable, happy times with loved ones and close friends. Someone is likely to need your help or advice, and you'll have to make time in your schedule to attend to this.

February (7 personal month): This is a time to plan, to think, and to wait patiently. It's not a time to assert yourself. Enjoy this quieter time and refuse to get involved in any arguments or disputes. Your energy levels will be lower than usual.

March (8 personal month): This is a busy, constructive month with the focus on money and finances. The hard work you put in now will be rewarded in the near future. Focus on what needs to be done and remain conscientious and disciplined, and you'll make the most of this month.

April (9 personal month): This is a good month to complete tasks and to make plans for the next few months. It's a good time for creative activities, and for helping people in your community.

May (1 personal month): This is an excellent month for starting new projects. Your enthusiasm and energy levels are high. Assert your independence and move forward now.

June (11 personal month): You'll need patience this month. As you'll feel more sensitive than usual, avoid arguments and stressful situations. Keep active and allow enough time for your projects to bear fruit. Make sure you don't spend too much time working on small, time-consuming tasks.

July (3 personal month): This is an excellent month to have fun and express yourself. You'll feel positive, outgoing, and ready for anything. You may choose to do something outrageous or different, purely to enjoy the reactions of others. Make the most of the light-hearted nature that this month provides, as you'll be busy again in August.

August (4 personal month): You'll need to be practical and well-organized this month. Be serious, conservative, punctual, and work to a plan. Make sure you handle home and family obligations. If you do the work that needs to be done, you'll make good progress this month.

September (5 personal month): This is a 5 month in a 5 year. This double-up increases the surprises, joys, and excitement of this unusual year. Expect the unexpected. You might take a trip or experiment with something you'd never considered doing before. You'll enjoy yourself and will grow from the experience.

October (6 personal month): This month gives you some idea of the duties and responsibilities you'll be dealing with next year. The focus is on home, family, and the community. You may have to limit your own activities because of the needs of others, especially someone close to you.

November (7 personal month): This is a month to focus on yourself and think carefully about your long-term future. It's a good time to look below the surface of things and make up your own mind on what you discover. It's not a month to push forward, and you'll get better results if you patiently wait until next month.

December (8 personal month): This is a busy month, and your hard work will prove worthwhile financially. You'll make some good decisions using your business and organizational skills. There'll be some interesting opportunities to consider, and you'll finish the year feeling positive about the future of you and your loved ones.

Six Personal Year

In a six year the focus is on home, family, duties, obligations, and the welfare of your community as a whole. This is a good year for getting on well with people and developing long-term relationships. You'll be involved in a variety of activities and will enjoy a busy and eventful year. Make sure to take time out to rest and relax, as you'll be tempted to overdo things. If relationships are going well, they'll continue to develop and grow. Tend to your relationships and spend as much time as possible with the people you love. You'll have a strong sense of responsibility this year. You're likely to be involved in beautifying your surroundings in some way this year, too.

January (7 personal month): This is a quieter introspective month that will find you soul-searching at times. You'll need to be disciplined, patient, and responsible this month. Take the opportunity for exercise. It'll be good for you and will give you a chance to think matters through.

February (8 personal month): The focus is on money and financial matters this month. It's an action month in which you'll have the opportunity to move ahead. You'll be focusing on the larger picture this month, but make sure you also pay attention to the details.

March (9 personal month): You'll be involved in helping others this month. Something is likely to end or come to a conclusion. This is a good time to make plans for the rest of the year. You'll need to be tolerant and compassionate and keep your feelings under control.

April (1 personal month): You'll be making changes and coming up with new ideas. These will probably relate to family and loved ones. Be caring and remain aware of other people's feelings and needs. Your working life will be busy, but make sure your loved ones are your primary focus.

May (2 personal month): You'll have to be patient and wait for results this month. As you'll be feeling more sensitive than usual, avoid arguments and think before speaking. You'll have the opportunity to create a more harmonious home and family life this month. Trust your intuition.

June (3 personal month): You'll be enjoying a good social life this month. This is an excellent month for making new friends and taking up new interests, particularly ones that make use of your creative abilities. There's also potential for enjoyable romantic times. Try to have a mini-vacation, or a few days off, this month if possible.

July (4 personal month): This is a month of slow, steady progress. You may feel that you're marking time or even sliding backward, but signs of progress will be evident by the end of the month. Keep focused on what you're doing, work steadily, make sure to take time off every now and again, and think about the rewards your hard work and effort will produce.

August (5 personal month): Your plans may change this month. Even so, it's a perfect month for a vacation or to travel. Try to visit places you haven't been to before and make friends with people with different and possibly unusual interests.

September (6 personal month): You'll be making some important family decisions this month. There'll be new responsibilities that you'll be happy to accept. Enjoy the pleasures of love, romance, and special family time. Appreciate the beauty all around you.

October (7 personal month): You'll feel the need for time by yourself to make plans for next year. This is a good month for inner growth, and you'll be developing spiritually and intuitively. It's also a good time to learn new skills, and you may decide to research something that interests you.

November (8 personal month): You'll be thinking about your money and financial goals. It's an excellent month for making plans and acting on them. You'll be full of energy and, although you'll be working hard, you'll enjoy every minute of it.

December (9 personal month): You'll be helping others in some way during this month. Be compassionate and understanding. This is a month of endings, and you'll be completing a number of tasks to free you up for the holiday season. You might receive some form of recognition.

Seven Personal Year

This is a quieter year that gives you the opportunity to explore some of the deeper meanings of life. You'll be learning more about yourself, too, while growing steadily in knowledge and wisdom. You may take up a new hobby or interest. You might become interested in technical projects. You may well become interested in spiritual and philosophical ideas. During this year you'll enjoy frequent quiet times on your own. This is a special nonmaterialistic year that brings its own special rewards and satisfactions.

January (8 personal month): The focus this month is on your finances, money, and organization. Do something constructive. Be patient as the pace of this month may not be as fast as you would like. This is an excellent month for buying and selling. Make sure everyone is happy with the transaction.

February (9 personal month): You'll be called upon to help in your local community. Some projects you've been working on will finish, and you'll be thinking about what you want to get underway next month.

March (1 personal month): This is a good month to start something you've been thinking about for some time. Use your intuition. You'll be enthusiastic and pre- pared to work hard. You may research or study a subject that is important to you. You'll feel positive and enthusiastic all month.

April (2 personal month): This is a slower month in which you may feel more sensitive than usual. You'll need to be patient and avoid arguments and pettiness. Make sure to get enough rest, as your energy levels will be lower than usual. Enjoy your close relationships.

May (3 personal month): You'll be socializing and enjoying yourself this month. You may do some entertaining or perhaps be entertained by others. Express your talents and your thoughts. Enjoy pleasant conversations with friends and family. You'll be feeling optimistic about everything going on in your life.

June (4 personal month): You'll need to be well-organized and practical this month. You'll make slow but steady progress. You may feel that you're doing most of the work and are not getting full recognition for your contribution. Correct any mistakes immediately, to prevent major problems later.

July (5 personal month): Your plans may change unexpectedly this month. Do something different simply for the fun of it. You're likely to investigate something you've never done before.

August (6 personal month): You'll be the peacemaker this month. Assume responsibility and keep the peace. Others may come to you for advice or a shoulder to lean on. The focus of this month is on home, family, and the wider community.

September (7 personal month): This is the most introspective month of this inward-looking year. You may feel slightly lonely at times, even though it's your choice to spend time on your own. Learn, think, meditate, and grow in knowledge and wisdom.

October (8 personal month): This month gives you an idea of the busy, exciting financial and commercial year you'll be experiencing next year. Research and investigate any opportunities that appeal to you. If you're willing to work, your fortunes are about to rise.

November (9 personal month): There'll be opportunities to help others this month, and you'll get great pleasure from this. This is a good month for making plans, but don't start anything major this month. Make sure that you see the overall picture and don't get lost in the details.

December (1 personal month): Move forward strongly. This is a busy month, but you'll still find time to get started on your ideas and projects. Seek advice from people you trust, and then act. Listen to your hunches and feelings. Aim high and create some ambitious plans.

Eight Personal Year

You'll feel ready to move ahead strongly and achieve some worthwhile goals this year. This will be a good year financially if you have a goal and work steadily toward achieving it. Money will flow in and out this year. Don't take any unnecessary risks. You'll need to be cautious, but progressive, to make the most of the opportunities this year offers.

January (9 personal month): You'll be starting the new year by finishing off anything that wasn't completed last year. Part of you will be looking back, but you'll also be making plans for what you want to achieve this year. This is a month of endings rather than beginnings.

February (1 personal month): You'll be moving forward again this month. Your energy and enthusiasm levels will be high, and you'll be full of ideas. Think them through carefully and act on the most promising ones.

March (11 personal month): This is a slower month that gives you the opportunity to pause, reflect, and make plans. Be patient and allow as much time as necessary to make an important decision. Even though you may feel frustrated or held back in some way, this month will give you a valuable opportunity to consolidate before moving ahead again.

April (3 personal month): This is a good month to meet people and make new friends. You'll have time for hobbies and interests, too. There'll be responsibilities that need to be attended to, but the focus of this month is pleasure.

May (4 personal month): This is a busy month and you'll be struggling to find time to do all the necessary practical, daily routine tasks. At times, you may feel as if you're working hard but not getting anywhere. However, by the end of the month you'll have a clearer idea of where you want to go.

June (5 personal month): Expect changes this month. Some will be planned and others will happen unexpectedly. Do something different purely for the fun of it. It's a good month for physical activities.

July (6 personal month): The focus this month is on your home and family life. You'll be called upon to provide valuable advice or help people who are close to you. Make the most of family activities.

August (7 personal month): This is a quieter, gentler month in this busy financial year. You'll want time by yourself to think, study, and analyze. Trust your intuition, and don't rely entirely on logic. You'll enjoy any activities that are mentally stimulating this month.

September (8 personal month): This is an important month in a busy, money-oriented year. You'll be making important decisions. Even though this is a busy month, make sure to allow time for rest and relaxation.

October (9 personal month): You'll have the opportunity to help others with the knowledge that you've learned. You could be doing some work in the community, but do it for your own satisfaction—you may not receive much gratitude or feedback. This is a good time to finish up some projects and think about new ones.

November (1 personal month): You'll be starting something new this month. You'll be enthusiastic and raring to go. Take time to lower your stress levels when necessary.

December (2 personal month): You'll be ready for a quieter month and will enjoy a pleasant holiday season with the special people in your life. You could be feeling more sensitive than usual. Be tactful and kind when dealing with others. Refuse to enter any arguments and instead concentrate on enjoying the festivities.

Nine Personal Year

This is the final year of your epicycle (the nine-year cycle of experience). You've learned a great deal during this time. There's a possibility that you'll receive some sort of recognition for something you've done during this year. You're also likely to be asked to help in your community during this year. As well as thinking about what you've achieved, you'll also be making forward plans. You'll have to decide what projects you want to take with you into the next epicycle.

January (1 personal year): You'll start the year with a great deal of energy and enthusiasm. You'll be working on some new ideas and will feel excited to be moving forward again. Enjoy the stimulation and excitement of this progressive month.

February (11 personal month): You'll be working on the details, rather than the overall picture, this month. Be patient and try to avoid emotionally difficult situations. Spend quiet time with family and friends.

March (3 personal month): You'll be feeling optimistic and on top of the world. Make the most of the social activities that occur this month. Enjoy pleasant times with friends and loved ones. Spend time on your creative interests and make the most of all the opportunities that come your way.

April (4 personal month): This is a busy, practical month. You'll be working hard, but your efforts will pay off if you're disciplined and well-organized.

May (5 personal month): Expect some surprises this month. This is an eventful time, and there are a few changes coming up. Be flexible and prepared to make changes at a moment's notice. You're likely to find yourself doing something you never thought you'd do this month.

June (6 personal month): There'll be new responsibilities this month. Your thoughts and energies will be focused on your home, family, and community. You may not be able to do all the things you want to because of the needs of others. Be prepared to both give and receive advice.

July (7 personal month): You'll seek out quiet times to be on your own this month. It's a good month for studying, investigating, and researching. Let the special people in your life know when you need time by yourself.

August (8 personal month): Money is the focus of this month, immediately following a month that is totally non-materialistic. This is a good month for all financial dealings. If you buy something, you'll get it for a good price; if you sell something, you'll receive a good price for it. Work hard and pay attention to the details.

September (9 personal month): You're likely to receive some recognition for your past actions. You'll be making decisions about future progress. There may be a few melancholy moments as you let go of things that have ceased to be important.

October (1 personal month): You'll be starting to make the changes that become increasingly important next year. You'll be feeling more positive about every aspect of your life and will start moving ahead again.

November (2 personal month): You'll experience some delays and frustrations this month. Accept them and enjoy this quieter month. Avoid anger and irritability, especially with family members. Be patient and express your gratitude when things come to you this month.

December (3 personal month): You'll finish the year feeling positive about the future. There'll be a sense of release, and you'll make the most of the holiday celebrations. Your imagination, sense of humor, and original ideas help you make this an exciting, fun-filled month.

Personal Days

In addition to personal years and months, it's also possible to look at personal days and even personal hours. In practice, I seldom look at personal hours, though I knew a numerologist many years ago in New Delhi who regularly told people what time of day was best to visit a dentist, go to the bank, or even buy groceries.

To find a personal day, all you need to do is add the day of the month to the person's personal month number and reduce the total to a single digit. A personal hour is worked out using a 24-hour clock. The personal day number is added to the hour, and again the total is reduced to a single digit.

When people ask for the best day on which to do something, I suggest that they:

Start anything on a 1 personal day.

Go shopping on a 1, 2, or 3 personal day.

Do something different, or take a chance on something, on a 5 personal day.

Buy something for the home or for a family member on a 6 personal day. It's also a good day to get married.

Attend spiritual or religious services on a 7 personal day. It's also a good time to study.

Make investment decisions and pay bills on an 8 personal day. It's also a good day to buy or sell anything.

Give gifts and make public appearances on a 9 personal day. This is also a good day to finish anything.

Spiritual Days

Spiritual days occur three or four times every month. These are positive days that a person can use to move ahead and undertake important tasks such as getting married, buying a house, traveling internationally, or making important financial decisions. As the name indicates, spiritual days are also good for any spiritual or religious activities. Years ago, someone told me that the traffic lights a person encounters all turn green on a spiritual day, and the person can take control and make things happen.

A spiritual day is derived from the calendar month, day, and year reduced to a single digit, or master number, and the person's life path number.

• • • EXERCISE ELEVEN • • •
How to Determine Spiritual Days

Again, we'll use Suzanne Roberts and her 8 life path number. Let's assume we're looking for her spiritual days in January 2025.

Month: 1

Day: 1

Year: 2025

1 + 1 + 2025 = 2027

2 + 0 +2 +7 = 11

This would be an important day for someone with an 11 life path number. However, as Suzanne's life path number is an 8, January 1, 2025, will be a typical day for her.

January 2, 2025, would be a 3 universal day. January 3 would be a 4 universal day, and so on. January 7 is the 8 universal day. As this is the same number as Suzanne's life path number, it is the first spiritual day of 2025 for Suzanne:

Month: 1

Day: 7

Year: 2025

1 + 7 + 2025 = 2033

2 + 0 + 3 + 3 = 8

The other spiritual days for Suzanne in January 2025 are January 16th and January 25th.

Here's another example. Let's assume we want to know Suzanne's spiritual days in July 2026.

Month: 7

Day: 1

Year: 2026

7 + 1 + 2026 = 2034

2 + 0 + 3 + 4 = 9

As July 1 is a 9 universal day, it means that Suzanne's first spiritual day this month will be eight days away on July 9th:

Month: 7

Day: 9

Year: 2026

7 + 9 + 2026 = 2042

2 + 0 + 4 + 2 = 8

Her other spiritual days this month will be on July 18th and 27th.

Chapter Thirteen
YOUR LUCKY NUMBERS

Throughout history, people have been interested in the idea of lucky numbers. It's not surprising, as most people have noticed that certain numbers seem to follow them through life, or at least for a lengthy period. They may have lived in a house numbered 60 for several years and then moved to another house with the same number. Maybe their parking spot at work is numbered 60 and they regularly catch a bus with the same number, too. Many people believe that when this occurs, it's a sign that the universe is giving them a lucky number.

Many people say a number is lucky when they notice that good things seem to happen when they use that number. If that's the case, they should continue using it.

Some numbers have always been considered lucky. Three is a good example; people often say, "third time's a charm." Even numbers can be divided and reduced in value, but odd numbers can't be reduced and are therefore considered luckier than even numbers. William Shakespeare referred to this in *The Merry Wives of Windsor* (act 5, scene 1, lines 3–5): "This is the third time; I hope good luck lies in odd numbers. There is divinity in odd numbers, either in nativity, chance, or death." And sixteen hundred years before Shakespeare was born, the Roman poet Virgil (70–19 BCE) wrote in his eighth *Eclogue*: "God delights in odd numbers."

The only odd number that isn't considered luckier than an even number is thirteen. However, gamblers, most of whom are highly superstitious, consider thirteen to be a lucky number. "Lucky thirteen" is a popular number to play, especially on a Friday the thirteenth.

However, each of the single-digit numbers are considered lucky in different ways:

One is considered a lucky number because it is indivisible and stands alone. When multiplied by itself, it remains the same. It symbolizes God, the sun, the intellect, purity, and the life force of creation. It also symbolizes masculine energy.

Two is considered a lucky number that symbolizes union. It also indicates balance in the universe, as it represents a wide range of opposites, such as male and female, good and evil, and life and death. It also symbolizes the mother and feminine energy.

Three has always been considered a lucky number. Pythagoras, the ancient Greek philosopher who modernized numerology 2,600 years ago, considered three to be the perfect number. Three symbolizes the miracle of birth, as a man and a woman create a child. It symbolizes birth, life, and death, as well as past, present, and future. We also have three cheers, three wishes, three strikes before you're out, and the third attempt at anything is "a charm."

Four is often said to be the luckiest even number, as many important things happen in fours. There are four seasons, four elements, four cardinal directions, four gospels, four evangelists, and four suits in the tarot deck and regular playing cards.

Five is considered lucky because people have five fingers on each hand and five toes on each foot. Ancient Greeks and Romans considered the number lucky, using the figure of a five-pointed star as a protective amulet.

Six is considered lucky, as the Bible says God created the world in six days and rested on the seventh. Six is said to be a lucky number for people who are honest but unlucky for dishonest people. People born on the sixth of the month are believed to be able to foretell the future.

Seven is considered a lucky number, as it is indivisible and unrelated to any other numbers from one to ten. The seventh son of a seventh son and the seventh daughter of a seventh daughter are considered extremely lucky. They're also said to have healing abilities and even the gift of second sight. The ancient Greeks considered it to be the perfect number, as it's the sum of the triangle and the square, which they considered to be perfect shapes. The phases of the moon change every seven days, there are seven days in a week and seven colors in a rainbow, and five planets, plus the sun and moon, are visible to the human eye. People are said to be in "seventh heaven" when they're blissfully happy. An ancient tradition says that if the sum of all the numbers in your date of birth is divisible by seven, you will be protected and lucky throughout life.

Eight is considered a lucky number for people seeking business and financial success. After the six days of creation and a seventh day of rest, the eighth day promises a better life in the world to come. Eight has always been considered a lucky number in China, as it is a sign of money coming soon and its pronunciation sounds similar to another word that means "to make a fortune." Traditionally, eight is said to be luckier for people over the age of fifty.

Nine is considered a lucky number, as it is the sum of three, a lucky number, multiplied by itself. It's also notable because no matter what number it is multiplied by, the sum of the digits in the total will always total nine. It is often associated with fertility, as pregnancy lasts for nine months. Cats are lucky, as they're said to have nine lives, someone who experiences a brief run of luck is called a nine-day wonder. A stitch in time can save nine, and a happy person is said to be on cloud nine.

Your most important and usually luckiest number is your life path number. You can use this number whenever you need a single number. You can also use any other numbers that can be reduced down to your life path number. If, for instance, your life path number is 5, you could also use 14, 23, 32, 41, 50, 59, 68, 77, 86, and 95, which all reduce to a 5. Master numbers are usually used as they are, without reducing them to a single digit. However, if your life path number is 11, you can also use any numbers that reduce down to this number. This gives you 29, 38, 47, 56, 65, 74, 83, and 92 that can be used as potential lucky numbers. This can't be done with a 22 life path, though, as there aren't any two-digit numbers that can be reduced to 22.

You can also use your expression, soul urge, and day of birth numbers, as well as multiples of them, as lucky numbers. Remember, though, that your life path is approximately 40 percent of your makeup, your expression 30 percent, your soul urge 20, and your day of birth 10 percent. This means that your life path number is likely to be twice as lucky as your soul urge number.

The number of your day of birth is an exception to this, and can be used as a lucky number, too, especially when you're looking for good luck on any matters involving your home and family. This includes parents, grandparents, siblings, children, and nieces and nephews. If your day of birth number has two digits, you can use them as they are or reduce them to a single digit, if you prefer.

You also have a lucky number for each year. This is your personal year number (see chapter 12). The activities and interests you'll be focused on during any year are indicated by your personal year number, making this a highly effective lucky number for the year.

The best time to use your lucky numbers is when one of your personal days happens to be the same number as your life path, expression, soul urge, or day of birth numbers. In fact, many people use their personal day number as their lucky number for that day.

Success Number

Another number that many people use as a lucky number is the success number. This number relates to the day of the month you were born on.

If you were born on the 1st, 5th, or 7th day of any month, your success number is 5. These days are the 1st, 5th, 7th, 10th, 14th, 16th, 19th, 23rd, or 28th of any month.

If you were born on the 2nd, 4th, or 8th day of the month, your success number is 8. These days are the 2nd, 4th, 8th, 11th, 13th, 17th, 20th, 22nd, 26th, 29th, or 31st of any month.

If you were born on the 3rd, 6th, or 9th day of the month, your success number is 6. These days are the 3rd, 6th, 9th, 12th, 15th, 18th, 21st, 24th, 27th, or 30th of any month.

Harmonious Days

Many people believe that they have good days and bad days. Numerology helps people determine the best days to perform different tasks. Bad days are caused by people's experiences and beliefs. If something negative happened to someone on the fifth of any month, for example, that person might come to believe that 5 is an unlucky number for them. In the Western world, 13 is considered an unlucky number, and it can be hard to find a high-rise building with a clearly labeled thirteenth floor. There's even a word to describe the fear of this number: triskaidekaphobia.

Fortunately, you can make every day as good as possible by working out your harmonious day numbers. This will let you know in advance the advantages, disadvantages, and possibilities any day has to offer.

• • • Exercise Twelve • • •
How to Determine Harmonious Days

Harmonious days are determined by adding the life path, expression, and full date of the day you want to evaluate and reducing the total down to a single digit.

We'll use our imaginary friend Suzanne Roberts as our example. We already know that her life path number is 8 and her expression number is 9. To determine her harmonious day for July 5, 2026, we create a sum using these three numbers.

Life path number: 8

Expression number: 9

Number of the day: 5

July: 7

5: 5

Year: 2026

7 + 5+ 2026 = 2038

2 + 0 + 3 + 8 = 13, and 1 + 3 = 4

Total: 8 + 9 + 4 = 21

Harmonious Day: 2 + 1 = 3

Suzanne will have a 3 harmonious day on July 5, 2026.

Here are the most favorable activities that can be done on each harmonious day.

1: This is an excellent day to progress and move ahead. Focus on one specific task or goal and complete it by the end of the day, if possible. It's a good day to investigate business opportunities and to make decisions about any practical matters.

2: This is a good day for making plans, and for thinking about problems and concerns. It's a good day for reflection and evaluation, but is not a good day to act, or to try to force a decision on any matter. Be patient, think quietly, and wait for a better day in which to act.

3: This is a positive day and you'll be able to combine business and pleasure. You may be involved in several activities, and any problems that occur will be solved quickly and easily. It's a good day for catching up with friends and having fun.

4: This is a busy day filled with routine tasks and responsibilities. You'll be focused on work and have little time for fun activities. If you stay motivated, you'll be pleased with the results of your efforts.

5: This is an exciting day and you're likely to try something new and different. Remain aware of your responsibilities, and don't grasp anything purely for the sake of change or variety. Opportunities are likely to come to you today. This is a good day to take a chance, but make sure you work out the odds first.

6: This is a good day for all interactions with others, especially the people you love. You'll enjoy all your social encounters. Try to see other people's points of view and avoid disagreements. This is a day of harmony and love.

7: This is a good day to study, learn, contemplate, and think about the deeper things in life. It's a good day for planning, for seeking advice, and for thinking philosophic thoughts. This is a day of mysteries and secrets, making this a lucky day for many people.

8: This is a good day for large-scale undertakings and for all financial activities. Focus on the larger picture, and don't be diverted by small problems. This is a busy day, but one with good opportunities for advancement and reward.

9: This is a good day for success and achievement, especially in creative areas. It's a day to announce bold plans, to celebrate your achievements, and to acknowledge everyone who has helped you achieve your goals. It's also a good day to express your generosity and love for humanity.

Multiple Lucky Numbers

There'll be times when you'll want more than one lucky number. Lotto numbers are an example. In New York, the lotto numbers range from 1 to 59, and you need to choose six numbers to participate. Let's assume your life path number is 3, and you're in an 8 personal year.

Start by writing down all the numbers below 59 that are numerologically connected with 3. These are 3, 12, 21, 30, 39, 48, and 57. Do the same with numbers that are numerologically connected with 8. These are 8, 17, 26, 35, 44, and 53. This gives you thirteen numbers to choose from. You might choose three numbers from each group to create a line in Lotto. You could choose the first three numbers from your life path: 3, 12, and 21, followed by the last three numbers from your personal year: 35, 44, and 53. This gives you: 3, 12, 21, 35, 44, and 53. You might alternate numbers from each group, and if necessary, place them in numerical order afterward. If you did that with the above numbers, you'd create: 3, 8, 12, 17, 21, 26.

You can create additional numbers by going through the same process with numbers derived from your soul urge and day of birth.

Another method is to use your full name. In numerology, your full name at birth is more important than any name changes that occur, such as when someone gets married or elects to change their name by deed poll. This system involves adding up the amount of letters in each name and using them individually, or by reducing them to a single digit. Here's an example:

7 + 5 + 6 = 18, and 1 + 8 = 9

Frances could use 9 as a lucky number. If she wanted three lucky numbers, she could use 7, 5, and 6. If she wanted more numbers, she could create lists of numbers that are numerologically connected with the 9, as well as 7, 5, and 6.

You can enhance the effectiveness of your lucky numbers by wearing, carrying, or even consuming the colors, gemstones, and herbs that relate to them (see chapter 1).

Chapter Fourteen
COMPATIBILITY

Compatibility is a vital factor in relationships that reveals how well the two people involved in a relationship get on together. Physical attraction is a good start, but true compatibility also requires similar values, beliefs, interests, goals, and love. This ensures both partners work together harmoniously most of the time. There also needs to be mutual emotional support, honesty, communication, acceptance of each other's shortcomings, and similar senses of humor.

No one needs help to recognize initial attraction, but many methods have been devised to help determine long-term compatibility. Of course, with love and goodwill on both sides, almost any relationship can be made to work. However, life is considerably easier if each person in the relationship has numbers that harmonize well with the other person's numbers.

There is one combination of numbers considered to be the best indicator of a successful relationship: when both people share a soul urge number. It's said that a couple with this combination live for each other, as their aims and goals are the same. Many people think that couples with the same soul urge number have been together in previous lifetimes.

Another strong indication of a long-lasting and successful relationship occurs when the two people have the same personal year number. When this happens, they automatically also have the same personal month and personal day numbers. Most couples have years where they share similar goals and others when they have vastly different aims. When the two people in a relationship have the same personal years, they're always heading toward the same goals. This fortunate occurrence happens when each person's day and month of birth add up to the same number. Here's an example. John was born on August 15. 8 + 1 + 5 = 14, and 1 + 4 = 5. Mary was born on December 20. 1 + 2 + 2 + 0 = 5. In 2026, both John and Mary will be in a six personal year. In 2027, they'll both be in a seven personal year, and they'll continue to share the same personal years throughout their lives.

Here's an example of a couple with different personal year numbers. Hamish was born on February 19 (2 + 1 + 9 = 12, and 1 + 2 = 3). Ava was born on November 12 (1 + 1 + 1 + 2 = 5). In 2026, and in most other years, they'll be focused on different matters. Hamish will be in a 4 personal year while Ava will be in a 6 personal year. This means that Hamish will be concerned with organization, efficiency, and hard work while Ava will be focused on home and family matters, home improvements, and spending time with loved ones and friends. Next year, 2027, Hamish will be in a 5 personal year, which means he'll want freedom, variety, and new opportunities. Ava will be in a 7 personal year and will want a quiet year to think, learn, and make plans for the future.

There's also a strong connection when the life path, expression, soul urge, or day of birth numbers of one person are the same as at least one of the other person's main numbers. In fact, this is probably what caused them to become attracted to each other in the first place. Someone with a life path number of 3, for instance, will be interested in someone who has a 3 as their life path, expression, soul urge, or day of birth number.

Here's an example. Jason has a 3 life path, an 8 expression, a 7 soul urge, and a 1 day of birth. Olivia has a 4 life path, a 3 expression, a 9 soul urge, and an 11 day of birth.

The number 3 is the only number Jason and Olivia have in common: Jason's life path and Olivia's expression. This gives them a point of connection.

Chapter Fifteen

NUMEROLOGY
IN EVERYDAY LIFE

Numerology can be extremely useful in everyday life. You can, for instance, make a quick assessment of someone using nothing but the first letter and first vowel in their first name. The interpretations of the first letter and vowel are slightly modified for this. A, J, and S all relate to number 1 (independence, assertiveness, leadership). However, A, being the first of these, is the most dynamic and ambitious of the three. J still has leadership qualities but is more cautious. S also can be a powerful leader but is the most emotional of the three letters.

B, K, and T (tact, diplomacy, cooperation) all relate to number 2. B is extremely sensitive and can be shy, reluctant, and indecisive. K is the eleventh letter of the alphabet and acts more like an 11 than a 2. It is intuitive, spiritual, and suffers from nervous tension. T relates well to others but suffers from anxiety. They're inclined to be extremely emotional.

C, L, and U (self-expression, creativity, joy) all relate to number 3. C is friendly, chatty, and seeks pleasure and enjoyment. L is friendly and sociable but thinks before acting. U is sensitive, indecisive, and doesn't always express its true feelings.

D, M, and V (hard work, system, and order) relate to the number 4. D is reliable, stable, disciplined, and hard working. M has all the qualities of D but finds it hard to express its feelings in words. V is the twenty-second letter of the alphabet and has leadership qualities along with the hard-working approach and attitude of the other two letters.

E, N, and W (freedom and variety) relate to number 5. E is adventurous, restless, adaptable, and versatile. It needs a great deal of freedom. N is like E but is more sensible and keeps its feet on the ground, thinking carefully before acting. W needs change and variety but tends to work more within limits than E and N. It is good at expressing itself verbally.

F, O, and X (responsibility and love) relate to the number 6. F often struggles, as it accepts too many responsibilities. It is sensitive, caring, and enjoys helping others. O accepts responsibilities well and rarely expresses its own feelings. It gives a great deal of itself to others. Like F and O, X is responsible and caring but experiences problems caused by its strong emotions and can be overwhelmed by them.

G, P, and Y (analysis, wisdom, and understanding) relate to 7. G has a good mind and is reserved and thoughtful. It works best on its own and is often nervous and unsure of itself. It enjoys analyzing and searching for hidden truths. P is similar but isn't as forceful or ambitious as a G. Y has an intense and perceptive mind. It enjoys gaining insights into philosophy and intuition. It also finds it hard to draw conclusions about this deep thinking.

H, Q, and Z (material success) relate to the number 8. H has good leadership skills and enjoys working in business fields. Q has the same capabilities as H but has a different, sometimes eccentric, approach to everything it does. Z has plenty of energy and the capability to inspire and motivate others.

I and R (humanitarianism) relate to the number 9. I is sympathetic, sensitive, idealistic, and creative. It has a good brain but is usually ruled by its emotions. R is selfless, idealistic, and a natural humanitarian with a strong desire to help others.

The first letter is called the cornerstone, and it reveals the person's natural approach to experiences and life itself. The first vowel reveals an important character trait.

Suzanne Roberts has a cornerstone of 1, as the first letter of her name is an S. This shows that she is independent, ambitious, and could handle a leadership role if she had to. However, her emotions might let her down at times.

Her first vowel is a U, which relates to a 3. She is fun-loving, indecisive, and a creative thinker. Although she is sensitive, she may not always express her true feelings.

These two letters show that her emotions can be problematic, and she sometimes chooses to conceal her real feelings.

House Numbers

Numerologists are regularly asked questions about house numbers, usually by people who are moving and want to know if the new house number will be good or bad for them. Fortunately, there are no good or bad house numbers. The house is its own entity. A 1 house, for instance, possesses 1 energy, just as a 7 house contains 7 energy. You can move into any house you wish as long as you're willing to cooperate with the house number.

If you're running a business from your home, a house that related to 8, such as 8, 17, 26, 35, 44, 53, 62, 71, 80, 89, or 98, would be useful for you. Likewise, if you're looking for a home for you and your family, a house that related to 6 would work well.

If you're a gregarious person with a busy and full social life, 7 might not be a good house number for you, but 3 would work well. Seven is a good house number for people who enjoy living on their own or who desire a great deal of peace and quiet. It's a good number for people who like to study and follow solitary interests.

Usually the best house for you is one that relates to your life path, expression, soul urge, or day of birth so that the energy of the house will be working for you and will help you achieve your desires. However, this kind of agreement isn't always possible, and you may find yourself living in a house with a number that doesn't relate to any of your main numbers. When this occurs, you need to harmonize and work with the nature of the house. If you do this, you'll find that your experience in the house will be a positive one. If you're not prepared to do that, you're likely to experience problems and difficulties.

Here are the interpretations for each house number:

1: This is a good home for people who are confident, independent, and enjoy being in control. You'll have opportunities to develop your leadership skills and progress in your career.

2: This is a good home for people who get on well with others and enjoy social activities. It's a warm, positive home for partnerships, cooperation, and any matters involving tact and diplomacy.

3: This is a good home for positive, creative, imaginative people who enjoy entertaining and being entertained by friends with similar hopes and dreams. It's a happy home that encourages self-expression in all its forms.

4: This is a good home for people who like to plan ahead, pay attention to details, and work hard to achieve their goals. It's a home that provides the potential for long-term financial success. There is fun in this house, especially involving family and neighbors.

5: This is a good home for people who enjoy freedom and variety. There'll be many unexpected changes and occurrences for the people who live here. It's important that these people take time out every now and again to relax and unwind.

6: This is a good home for people who desire a strong home and family life. It can be a home that radiates generosity, love, and responsibility and care for others. It provides comfort, security, and ultimate material satisfaction.

7: This is a good home for peace, refinement, intellectual pursuits, and spiritual growth. It's a good home for people who enjoy living on their own or with one or two like-minded people.

8: This is a good home for people who have specific goals and know where they are going in life. This is often a home where business is conducted or is at least regularly discussed. It's a good home for financial growth, though it is likely to happen over time rather than overnight.

9: This is a good home for compassionate, tolerant, philanthropic, humanitarian people. It also provides a safe haven for people involved in the arts who create beauty and enjoyment with what they do.

Chapter Sixteen
ANGEL NUMBERS

Angel numbers are a form of divine guidance. They're sequences of numbers that appear apparently randomly in our lives but capture our attention because they occur on a regular or semi-regular basis. They're usually repeated numbers. You might, for instance, look at your watch and see the time is 2:22. A short time later, you park your car and notice you've parked outside a building numbered 222. Later, you receive $2.22 in change after making a purchase, and on your way home you notice you're following a car with 222 on its license plate. If this continues to occur, the chances are that this number will be important to you for some reason. It's rare for single numbers to be angel numbers; we all see numerous single numbers every day, making it difficult for a particular single number to be picked out as an angel number. Most angel numbers are two, three, or four digits long.

Angel numbers can appear in other forms, such as 789 or 3636. The common factor is that the same numbers appear repeatedly. At first, seeing them might seem purely coincidental, but after a while you'll realize that synchronicity must be involved and the numbers are sending you a message.

Sometimes angel numbers appear regularly for a while and are then never seen again. Other angel numbers might appear throughout a person's lifetime. There's no knowing how or when they appear, but the fact that they're noticed indicates that they're being shown for a reason.

As angel numbers are not connected to any of the numbers in a numerology chart, many people believe that they come from angels, angel guides, or some other spiritual source. No matter where they come from, angel numbers are always helpful and provide evidence that you are on track and here for a reason.

The first step in working with angel numbers is to pay attention whenever you come across one. It can be helpful to record these in a journal so that you quickly become aware of the angel numbers that repeat frequently.

You can interpret angel numbers individually or as a group, using their numerological meanings. If you frequently see the number 438, for instance, you could use the numerological meanings for 4, 3, and 8 individually. You might create a phrase or sentence that shows how the individual numbers work together. Alternatively (or in addition), you can pause and ask yourself how you feel whenever you see this number. It might be helpful to make a few notes about any thoughts or ideas that come into your mind, too.

At these times, it's likely you'll also connect with your intuition. Pause for a minute or two to see what message or lesson comes into your mind.

Set aside some time to reflect on the angel messages you've received and determine how they relate to what is going on in your life. It's possible that they relate to your hopes and dreams about your future. Record any insights you receive in your journal. Write down your thoughts and emotions, too. It can be useful to do this at the same time every day, as regularity will encourage the messages to start coming almost as soon as you sit down.

Here are the meanings for the most common angel numbers:

When a zero or a series of zeroes appears, it's a sign that different and fresh opportunities are coming up for you. You need to be alert, curious, and open to new and different ideas to make the most of this angel number.

The number one is a powerful indication that you're on the verge of a breakthrough. This is a good time to examine your goals, evaluate opportunities, and start moving forward. Right now, the universe is supporting you and your dreams. Two ones can also be interpreted as the master number 11, and the message is to act rather than think about what you might do.

Two or a series of twos appear when you're starting a period of making plans and working cooperatively with others. You'll need to be patient; anything worthwhile takes time and effort. The planning you do now will pay off in time. Two also relates to love and indicates that a relationship is growing and developing. Two twos can be interpreted as the master number 22, whose message is to aim high and start working toward your dreams.

A series of threes is a sign of opportunity and good luck. This is a good time to focus on your creative skills and talent with words. You'll be able to use your communication abilities to progress in all areas of your life.

If you start noticing four or a series of fours, it's a sign that you're building a good foundation that will help you progress more quickly in the future. Building this foundation usually involves a great deal of hard work in the short term, but all this effort ultimately pays off.

Five or a series of fives is a sign that some important changes are coming up. These changes offer excitement and new opportunities. This is usually a busy time, and you need to be quick to seize and act on the opportunities they offer.

The number six or a series (even 666) shows that you must nurture yourself as well as others. You need to find balance in your life and be as kind, understanding, and compassionate as possible. Sixes always relate to love and close relationships. Don't forget to love yourself as you do others. Self-love is vitally important. Sixes also provide healing energy to every area of your life.

The number seven or a series of sevens shows that your spirituality is growing and expanding. It's the perfect time to deepen your connection with the Divine. Seven can be a lucky number, too, which means you may be able to progress financially at this time by combining your spirituality with your values.

The number eight or a series of eights shows that you're about to receive more abundance in your life. This usually includes financial abundance, but can also mean an abundance of love, friendships, time, or happiness. Eight is a powerful number and gives you the opportunity to create the abundance you desire.

The number nine or a series of nines shows that you're completing a phase in your life and it's time to let go of past grievances, heal yourself, and start thinking about where you want to go from here.

As mentioned before, angel numbers don't have to be a repetition of the same number. For instance, if you see the number 7412 repeatedly, chances are that it is an angel number, and it's important, as it's been created solely for you. You can interpret these by looking at each number individually as well as adding them and reducing them to a single digit.

Remember that angel numbers are not the only way to receive guidance. Hunches, feelings, dreams, prayers, and a sense of knowing are just a few of the many ways that we can receive divine guidance. Accept angel numbers with gratitude and evaluate them carefully—they're likely to be gentle motivational messages from the universe.

CONCLUSION

I hope you now know more about yourself and where you're going in this lifetime than you did when you first picked up this book. At times, we all wonder if we're following the right path in life. Numerology is a practical system that enables us to recognize and use our strengths to our best advantage. It reveals talents and abilities you may not have discovered yet. It provides your purpose in life. It also indicates areas that you need to work on.

Numerology will keep you on track and provide guidance on when it is best to be patient and wait, and when to move forward.

Numerology will also help you in all your dealings with others. Even when you know nothing more than someone's first name, you'll have clues as to how you can best relate to the other person.

Numerology can also increase your popularity. Once people become aware of your interest in numerology, they'll ask you to draw up charts for them. It's wonderful to be able to help others in this way. A side benefit of this is that the more charts you erect for others, the more intuitive you'll become. Insights will come to you that may not seem to relate directly to the numbers you're analyzing but prove helpful and accurate.

Pythagoras is said to have proclaimed that "number is the within of all things," "all things are numbers," and "the beauty of numbers is that they are the purest form of truth" more than 2,600 years ago, though none of his writings have survived. However, every time you construct a chart for others, you'll discover a little more of the truth in those words.

It was an unforgettable day for me when I was first introduced to numerology. I hope this book has excited you and will encourage you to learn more about numerology. I also hope it will be the start of a life-long passion that will enable you to help yourself and others.

RECOMMENDED READING

LUCKENBILL, DANIEL. *Ancient Records of Assyria and Babylonia.* Vol. 2. University of Chicago Press, 1927.

TEGMARK, MAX. *Our Mathematical Universe: My Quest for the Ultimate Nature of Reality.* Alfred A. Knopf, 2014.

WEBSTER, RICHARD. *Chinese Numerology.* Llewellyn Publications, 1998.

WEBSTER, RICHARD. *Discovering Numerology.* Brook-
field Press, 1983.

WEBSTER, RICHARD. *Numerology Magic.* Llewellyn
Publications, 1998.

Notes

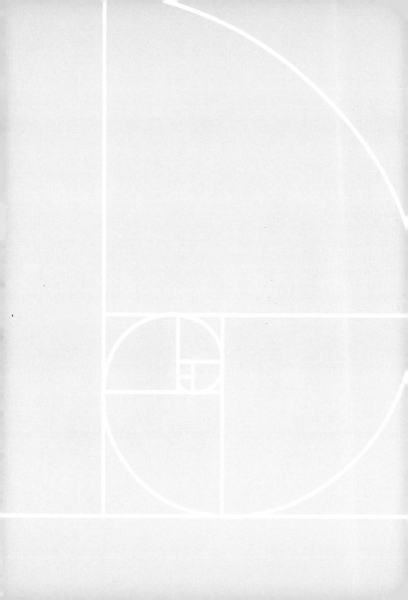